David

W9-DGP-838

K'zoo

May '86

Telling Classical Tales

Telling Classical Tales

Chaucer and the
Legend of Good Women

Lisa J. Kiser

Cornell University Press

ITHACA AND LONDON

Cornell University Press gratefully acknowledges a grant from the Andrew W. Mellon Foundation that aided in bringing this book to publication.

First published 1983 by Cornell University Press.
Published in the United Kingdom by
Cornell University Press, Ltd., London.

International Standard Book Number 0-8014-1601-9
Library of Congress Catalog Card Number 83-45135
Printed in the United States of America
*Librarians: Library of Congress cataloging information appears
on the last page of the book.*

The paper in this book is acid-free and meets the guidelines for permanence and durability of the Committee on Production Guidelines for Book Longevity of the Council on Library Resources.

For my father, Phil Kiser,
and my brother, Mark

Contents

Preface

In writing this book about Chaucer's *Legend of Good Women*, I have aimed to explain, as precisely as possible, the issues that Chaucer intended his poem to raise. One might want to argue that those issues are patently obvious, that the poem was written as comic atonement for the author's amatory "sins" in the *Troilus* and as another literary treatment of forsaken lovers, a subject that seems to dominate Chaucer's early verse. But to view the *Legend* as a poem about these issues only is to restrict one's vision to what are, for Chaucer, the work's means and devices, not its real ends. That is, the *Legend's* ostensible subject, love, is not its real subject at all. Rather, the poem was written to set forth some of Chaucer's basic views about literature: its sources, its usefulness, its forms, its audience, and its capacity to represent Christian truth.

As my title indicates, I have come to realize that the *Legend of Good Women* is most urgently concerned with Chaucer's interest in classical narrative. The *Legend* is one of those works (like the *Book of the Duchess*, the *House of Fame*, *Troilus and Criseyde*, and the *Knight's Tale*) that have much to say to us about the usefulness of classical literature in a Christian world and about how Chaucer wished to respect the integrity of his pagan sources even while transforming them into new, "medievalized" works of art. Yet in the course of expressing his views on classical art, the poet addresses other related issues as well. He shows, for example, that the relationship between literature and Christian truth is a very complex one and that a poem's genre and audience significantly affect its success in conveying truth. But the *Legend* does not offer up these views to its readers in any clear, straightforward manner. Instead, its thickly ironic texture and its broad comedy conceal Chaucer's intentions. The *Legend* is indeed a rich and challenging poem, one that deserves more critical attention than it has been granted.

My critical approach is, for the most part, historical in nature. That is, I have consistently tried to support my argument with evidence that was available to Chaucer or to any fourteenth-century man of letters. Terms and distinctions drawn from more recent theories of literary form, genre, and audience are not imposed upon Chaucer's poem, but are given space only in the notes and only as modern parallels to Chaucer's own critical thought. Finally, a word must be said here concerning my citations from the two surviving versions (called F and G) of Chaucer's Prologue to his *Legend*. Unless otherwise specified, I quote from the F text. After each quotation, I cite not only the line numbers of that text but also, where applicable, the line numbers of the corresponding passage in G.

It is a pleasure to express my gratitude to those who assisted me in the preparation and completion of this project. To the Houghton Mifflin Company and Oxford University Press I am grateful for permission to quote extensively from *The Works of Geoffrey Chaucer*, edited by F. N. Robinson, © F. N. Robinson, 1957 and 1961. To Diether H. Haenicke, dean of the College of Humanities at the Ohio State University, I owe my thanks for providing me with the precious gift of time in the form of a Special Research Assignment. To my department chairman, Julian Markels, I am also greatly indebted for support and encouragement. For kindly reading this book in typescript and offering many wise suggestions, I thank Alan Brown, Hoyt Duggan, Donald Howard, Stanley Kahrl, Charles

Wheeler, William Wilson, Christian Zacher, and—with particular gratitude—the readers and staff of Cornell University Press. To V. A. Kolve, with whose guidance I first began to read and understand Chaucer, I owe an especially large debt; to him I offer my deepest respect. Last of all, but first in my thoughts, is James Battersby, whose generosity, both emotional and intellectual, informs every page.

LISA J. KISER

Columbus, Ohio

Abbreviations

AHDLMA	*Archives d'histoire doctrinale et littéraire du moyen âge.* Paris.
EETS	Early English Text Society, original series.
EETS e.s.	Early English Text Society, extra series.
JEGP	*Journal of English and Germanic Philology*
MLN	*Modern Language Notes*
MLR	*Modern Language Review*
MP	*Modern Philology*
PL	J. P. Migne, ed. *Patrologiae cursus completus. Series Latina.* 221 vols. Paris: J. P. Migne, 1844–65.
RES	*Review of English Studies*
SATF	Société des anciens textes français. Paris.
SP	*Studies in Philology*
TLL	*Thesaurus Linguae Latinae.* Leipzig, 1806–9.

Telling Classical Tales

Introduction

One of the primary goals of poets living in the late medieval period was to create new and suitable vehicles for what they knew to be poetry's most important concern—namely, the transmission of wisdom bequeathed to them by the literature of their classical forebears. The challenge this task presented to medieval Christian artists had always been formidable, largely, of course, because of major philosophical differences between pagan and Christian cultures, not the least of which was a profound disparity between classical and medieval assumptions concerning the structure and governance of the world. Often alien in purpose to medieval audiences, much classical literature was absorbed only gradually into medieval culture, some of it being admitted formally only after certain theoretical advances of the twelfth-century humanists—including new theories of allegory—had begun to stretch Christian principles of acceptability enough to include many of those texts that treated pagan topics openly. And even after the groundwork had been laid by the innovative twelfth-century thinkers, it took the industry of practical people living in the following two centuries to develop and refine poetic strategies that enabled them to employ in their own poems the narratives that medieval culture had inherited from the Roman *auctores*. How Christian poets, from the beginnings of the medieval period to the Renaissance, transformed their literary heritage into useful Christian art has indeed become an increasingly well documented chapter of western intellectual history.

By the time Chaucer was writing, medieval artists had, of course, fully accepted the idea that classical stories could be useful to Christian readers. It was thus not necessary for Chaucer to direct his energy toward a defense of medieval classicism, for by his lifetime, defenses had already been made. But he was faced with the equally difficult task of solving some of the practical problems that inevitably arose when medieval Christian poets attempted to use classical materials within the structures of their own creations. If a classical narrative, for example, did not clearly present a moral, or did not present one that conformed to Christian standards, the medieval artist had to moralize (or remoralize) his material, especially if he saw the moral imperative as one of literature's most important functions. Or, when two versions of a narrative had been preserved (such as Ovid's and Virgil's differing accounts of the Dido/ Aeneas affair), the artist had to decide which version should be retold and why. Or, if the authoritative viewpoints of the Roman poets contradicted a Christian belief, the artist had to reconcile these perspectives, maintaining, as best he could, respect for his sources. To state the problem quite generally, medieval artists were faced with the burden of translating ancient issues into terms that could most immediately meet the needs of their own very different age.

Chaucer's poetry confronts all of these problems directly. Especially in his early years as a poet, Chaucer experimented extensively with the voices of his classical forebears, trying out various methods by which he could integrate his own creative material with that which he derived from careful study of the Latin poets. Even in his earliest major work, the *Book of the Duchess*, we find him relying heavily on Ovid's tale of Ceyx and Alcione to help him express his own views on art. In the same poem, as if to acknowledge this dependence on his literary past, Chaucer describes his chamber windows as adorned with sunlit images drawn from books on Troy and from classical tales of love. Thus, implies Chaucer, Roman art is inextricably linked with the light that fills the "room of dreams," the place where all of a poet's work begins. Similarly, in the *House of Fame* and the *Parliament of Fowls*, episodes and images from antiquity form backdrops for Chaucer's original plots. *Troilus and Criseyde*, too, is concerned with the relationship of classical fiction to Christian art, for this poem's power at times wholly depends on Chaucer's self-conscious juxtaposition of Christianity and paganism.

But the poem that best articulates Chaucer's attitudes toward his Roman masters is the *Legend of Good Women*, a work concerned with the act of telling classical tales in a much more direct (yet at the same time more complicated) way than the poems that predate it. For example, the *Legend*'s Prologue, though depending heavily on courtly convention, is nonetheless significantly indebted to the literature of the ancient world, its main characters being Cupid (Christianized though he is) and Alcestis of Thessaly, the self-sacrificing wife of classical mythology. The legends that follow the Prologue are also classical—at least in subject matter if not always in spirit. Yet this poem's important relationship to Chaucer's classicism has not been fully understood (or even recognized) because the *Legend* does not present its issues in any clear, discursive manner. Readers of the *Legend of Good Women* are faced with a work that is uncommonly perplexing and that covers much more ground than seems necessary to define and solve any classical "problems." The *Legend*'s courtly and Christian elements have dominated critical discussion of this work—surely because they seem to dominate the poem itself. But critics are now beginning to realize that the *Legend* must be read with its classical sources firmly in mind.[1]

[1] For the *Legend*'s debt to courtly literature of the fourteenth century, see John Livingston Lowes, "The Prologue to the *Legend of Good Women* as Related to the French Marguerite Poems, and the *Filostrato*," *PMLA*, 19 (1904), 593–683; William G. Dodd, *Courtly Love in Chaucer and Gower* (Boston: Ginn, 1913), pp. 208–32; Robert M. Estrich, "Chaucer's Prologue to the *Legend of Good Women* and Machaut's *Le Jugement dou Roy de Navarre*," *SP*, 36 (1939), 20–39.

In addition to the problems raised by the *Legend*'s complex amalgam of courtly, Christian, and classical material, this poem presents the reader with other obstacles to interpretation as well. Although it contains many features we have come to recognize as typical of Chaucer's imagination—a comical, self-effacing narrator, a chaotic dream world composed of fragments drawn from works by Chaucer's predecessors, a concern with love's uneven course in human affairs, and an easily discernible attitude of irreverence toward many commonly held beliefs— this poem nevertheless seems to defy all easy explanations of its significance. Its readers find themselves routinely faced with difficult problems of interpretation which seem to surround nearly every aspect of the work. First, because Chaucer left us with two versions of his poem's Prologue, scholars have been charged with the task of deciding which version was the poet's final one—and why.[2] Second, because Chaucer seems, in one version, to dedicate the poem to his queen, scholars have had to work with the possibility that the *Legend* was commissioned by her or was from the first intended to be topical in nature.[3] Finally, like some of Chaucer's other works, the *Legend* is incomplete, making any conclusive interpretation of it difficult.

For the *Legend*'s Christian elements, see, for example, D. D. Griffith, "An Interpretation of Chaucer's *Legend of Good Women*," in *Manly Anniversary Studies* (Chicago: Univ. of Chicago Press, 1923), pp. 32–41; William Allan Neilson, *The Origins and Sources of the Court of Love*, Studies and Notes in Philology and Literature, 6 (Boston: Ginn, 1899), p. 145; and Robert O. Payne, *The Key of Remembrance: A Study of Chaucer's Poetics* (New Haven: Yale Univ. Press, 1963), pp. 107–9. For Chaucer's attitude toward the classical material in his *Legend*, see Robert Worth Frank, Jr., *Chaucer and the Legend of Good Women* (Cambridge, Mass.: Harvard Univ. Press, 1972), pp. 28–36, and John M. Fyler, *Chaucer and Ovid* (New Haven: Yale Univ. Press, 1979), pp. 96–123. Source studies dealing with the individual legends will be cited in Chapter 4.

[2] On the Prologue's two versions, see especially Lowes, "The Prologue to the *LGW* as Related to the French Marguerite Poems," pp. 658–83, and "The Prologue to the *Legend of Good Women* in Its Chronological Relations," *PMLA*, 20 (1905), 749–864; Robert K. Root, ed., *Troilus and Criseyde* (Princeton, N.J.: Princeton Univ. Press, 1926), pp. xiv, lxx–lxxx; and Robert M. Estrich, "Chaucer's Maturing Art in the Prologues to the *Legend of Good Women*," *JEGP*, 36 (1937), 326–37. Payne, however, believes that the methods used to date the two versions are unreliable (p. 92).

[3] On the *Legend* and Queen Anne, see Lowes, "The Prologue to the *LGW* as Related to the French Marguerite Poems," pp. 666–76; Bernard L. Jefferson,

Even if readers did not have to face the *Legend*'s differing versions, its historical contexts, or its incompleteness, there would still remain the significant problem of how to define the poem's place in Chaucer's poetic development. If scholars are correct in their hypotheses, the two versions of the *Legend*'s Prologue were written in 1386 and 1394—that is, after the *Troilus* and shortly before and during the early composition of the *Canterbury Tales*. The *Legend* is thus a poem written in Chaucer's maturity and one he considered important enough to warrant the kind of extensive revision that must certainly have interrupted his work on the more ambitious project at hand—the writing of the *Tales*. Yet the poem at first seems to represent a step backward for Chaucer, as Robert Worth Frank, Jr. has noted, for it assumes the dream vision form he had abandoned earlier in favor of the *Troilus*'s purely narrative mode, and it takes up again the subject of love, a subject Frank suggests had been "exhausted" in the *Troilus* and essentially dropped in the early stages of the *Canterbury Tales*.[4] In fact, the *Legend*'s problematic place in Chaucer's poetic development is what prompted Frank to write what is our only full-length study of this poem, and he concludes that the *Legend* shows us a poet in training for the *Canterbury Tales*. Chaucer learns two things by writing his legendary: to manipulate "new matter" (classical stories) and to master the short form (one marked by selectivity and *brevitas*). Both of these "lessons," argues Frank, were useful to the poet in his later masterpiece.[5]

These conclusions, though intriguing, nonetheless provoke

"Queen Anne and Queen Alcestis," *JEGP*, 13 (1914), 434–43; George L. Kittredge, "Chaucer's Alceste," *MP*, 6 (1908–9), 435–39; and Samuel Moore, "The Prologue to Chaucer's 'Legend of Good Women' in Relation to Queen Anne and Richard," *MLR*, 7 (1912), 488–93. For speculation on other historical identities for the *Legend*'s characters, see Frederick Tupper, "Chaucer's Lady of the Daisies," *JEGP*, 21 (1922), 293–317; Margaret Galway, "Chaucer's Sovereign Lady: A Study of the Prologue to the *Legend* and Related Poems," *MLR*, 33 (1938), 145–99; Bernard F. Huppé, "Historical Allegory in the Prologue to the *Legend of Good Women*," *MLR*, 43 (1948), 393–99; and Walter E. Weese, "Alceste and Joan of Kent," *MLN*, 63 (1948), 474–77.
[4]Frank, pp. 3–4, 6, 12.
[5]Frank, pp. 169–87.

other questions concerning the *Legend*'s status as a mature poem, one written between the *Troilus* and the *Tales*. First, if Chaucer were merely learning to handle classical material in the *Legend*, what are we to say about his classical achievements in the *Troilus*, and why would he then virtually ignore his classical masters when he came to the *Canterbury Tales*? Also, why would he choose the short exemplum form for his *Legend*'s narratives, when at this point in his career he was working with longer narrative forms, such as those he adopted in *Troilus and Criseyde* and the *Knight's Tale*? And why would the radical *brevitas* he was supposedly mastering in the legends appear later merely as the ridiculous parodies in the *Monk's Tale*, which is composed of stories that are travesties of what narrative ought to be? Clearly, attempts to make the *Legend* easily bridge the gap between the *Troilus* and the *Canterbury Tales* are thwarted by the fact that the *Legend* is very much a backward looking poem, a work that seems to drag up the past rather than herald the future. This is, after all, the poem in which we find the famous catalogue of Chaucer's previous works, some written, as Alceste remarks, "goon ys a gret while."

Formal and chronological problems aside, there still remains the most challenging obstacle of all to readers of Chaucer's *Legend*, the task of sorting out and interpreting the complex layers of irony this poem so effectively manipulates. It would seem that by now, after benefiting from the writings of innumerable scholars and critics on the subject of Chaucer's wit, we would all be expert in the art of understanding the poet's jokes, but unfortunately, such a happy result has not come to pass. Because it is characteristic of Chaucer to treat even the most serious matters in comic fashion and because issues that appear to be his major concerns often turn out to be elaborate jokes, the real difficulty in reading and understanding his works is locating Chaucer himself in the tangled web of irony that usually conceals him. Most Chaucerians, even seasoned ones, still find themselves struggling to pinpoint the poet's true relationship with many of the characters and events in his works. In the *Legend* alone, modern critics have articulated radically contradictory interpretations of Chaucer's attitude toward Alceste, one of the *Legend's* main characters, and toward the classical stories that make up the legendary itself. Some critics judge Alceste to be obdurate and surly; others are convinced of her compassion and wit. Similarly, some see the stories as solemn examples of fourteenth-century classicism; others see them as comical travesties intended, among other things, to mock the ladies whose stories they tell.[6] It may be hard to believe that one poem is able to occasion these interpretive extremes or that evidence for such contradictory readings can be uncovered within the confines of a single work, but the *Legend of Good Women* confronts us with a Chaucer so refined and elusive that such extremes are possible even within the experience of a single reader over a period of time. Indeed this poem, however one interprets it, is a work that severely tries its readers' patience with irony.

The poem's plot is rather simple. Chaucer the narrator, after making some preliminary remarks about the value of learning things from sources other than direct experience, professes his devotion to books and then admits to a greater love—veneration of the daisy. Surrounded by a springtime landscape, the narrator describes his flower and shortly thereafter falls asleep, entering the dream world where the rest of the poem takes place. He meets the God of Love, who accuses him of "breaking love's law" in the *Troilus* and in his translation of the *Roman de la Rose*. Accompanying this deity is Alceste, who seems to be identified both with the narrator's daisy and with

[6]On Alceste, for example, compare John Gardner's statement that she is "almost as fierce as the god," *The Poetry of Chaucer* (Carbondale: Southern Illinois Univ. Press, 1977), p. 207, with Robert O. Payne's comment that she is "the intercessor for a sinner whose case requires that justice be tempered with mercy," *Key of Remembrance*, p. 107. See also H. C. Goddard's attack on Alceste's character in "Chaucer's *Legend of Good Women*," *JEGP*, 7 (1908), 108–9. On the stories as serious works, see Frank, p. 210; J. L. Lowes, "Is Chaucer's *Legend of Good Women* a Travesty?" *JEGP*, 8 (1909), 513–69; Robert K. Root, *The Poetry of Chaucer* (Boston: Houghton Mifflin, 1922), pp. 145–46; Dodd, pp. 215, 218, 231; and F. N. Robinson, ed., *The Works of Geoffrey Chaucer* (Boston: Houghton Mifflin, 1957), p. 482. On the stories as parodies, see John Fyler, pp. 98–115; Robert Max Garrett, "'Cleopatra the Martyr' and Her Sisters," *JEGP*, 22 (1923), 64–74; and Goddard, "Chaucer's *Legend of Good Women*," p. 101.

Alcestis of Thessaly, whose name she bears. She is briefly praised by a group of ladies who attend her, and then she manages to placate the angry God of Love by suggesting that the narrator do penance for his crimes. It is determined that since he spoke about faithless women in his two previous works, restitution might be possible through his composition of some stories about good women who were constant in love. The narrator complies, leaving us with an incomplete series of brief narratives that tell stories, all from classical sources, of ten ladies who suffered at the hands of faithless men.[7]

The key to understanding the Legend of Good Women, both Prologue and stories, lies in the full comprehension of the roles played by Chaucer's two main characters, Alceste and the God of Love. Nearly every reader of Chaucer's Legend has been amused by the God of Love. His contemptuous treatment of the poet-narrator, his ex cathedra judgments of Chaucer's past efforts, and his pretentious demands for retribution all make him a fully realized comic figure, perhaps the best since the learned eagle of the House of Fame. Yet it would be wrong merely to dismiss the God of Love as a comic foil, even though he is the vehicle for much of Chaucer's irony. First, the God of Love unites the erotic pagan world with the Christian tradition, thus placing this poem in the mainstream of love allegories that use religious symbolism in their treatment of secular love. Second, as I shall prove, the Legend's most important concern—to set forth Chaucer's beliefs about how classical fiction should be used—is tied up with what this deity has to say about literature.

[7]This summary of the poem's action accords with both versions of the Prologue. There are a few major structural disparities between the two, however, the most important being the different points at which the narrator falls asleep. In F, he actually experiences the birds' singing about the fowler's snares; in G, he dreams about it. The other important difference between the two versions involves the little "balade" that both Prologues include. In F, it is composed and sung by the narrator; in G, it is recorded as the praising ladies deliver it. The rest of the differences between F and G involve descriptive passages and dialogue. I will quote from the F Prologue and cite the corresponding lines in the G Prologue, noting when there is a significant difference between them. In general, however, I agree with Payne, who notes that the two Prologues do not differ in the attitudes they express toward the problems of poetry. See The Key of Remembrance, p. 92.

He presents us with a well-articulated critical theory that Chaucer intended us to examine closely, for only in discovering the God of Love's literary assumptions can we attend to the real issues that Chaucer's *Legend* addresses. The God of Love thus represents a typical Chaucerian enigma in that understanding him involves reconciling the poet's outrageous comedy with what are ultimately his serious concerns.

Alceste's meaning and identity are also not easily determined. To be sure, she exhibits attributes drawn from many different female authority figures of the kind so often encountered in medieval visionary poetry. However, as is made clear in the predream action and in the dream that follows it, she is first and foremost a daisy, rewarded with our narrator's loyal and passionate devotion. As John L. Lowes convincingly proved, Chaucer's decision to make his "lady" an unpretentious daisy has its origins in the fashionable *marguerite* poetry of his French contemporaries. Machaut, Deschamps, and Froissart all wrote poems extolling the daisy's special beauty and healing power, often comparing each of the flower's parts (root, stem, and flower) with a Christian virtue and then associating the daisy with the ladies from whom they wished to gain favor.[8] There can be no doubt that Chaucer is participating in the *marguerite* tradition by choosing a daisy as his lady, but we must not fail to note the significant difference between Chaucer's

[8]The daisies of these Frenchmen most often represent real female acquaintances named "Marguerite," a name common in fourteenth-century France. Machaut's *Dit de la fleur de lis et de la Marguerite*, for example, was probably written to celebrate the royal wedding between Phillippe of Burgundy and Marguerite of Flanders, and his *Dit de la Marguerite* contains references to Pierre of Cyprus, whose lady's name was Marguerite. For a fuller account of these poems, see James I. Wimsatt, *The Marguerite Poetry of Guillaume de Machaut*, University of North Carolina Studies in the Romance Languages and Literatures, no. 87 (Chapel Hill: Univ. of North Carolina Press, 1970), pp. 41–2, 50–59. For works of French daisy poetry that clearly allegorize the flower, see Froissart's *Dittié de la Margherite*, in *Oeuvres de Froissart: Poésies*, ed. Auguste Scheler, 3 vols. (Brussels, 1870–72), 2:209–15; Machaut's *Dit de la Marguerite*, in *Oeuvres de Guillaume de Machaut*, ed. Prosper Tarbé (Paris, 1849), pp. 123–29; and Deschamps's "Eloge d'une Dame du Nom de Marguerite," in *Oeuvres complètes de Eustache Deschamps*, ed. le marquis de Queux de Saint-Hilaire and Gaston Raynaud, SATF, 11 vols. (Paris, 1878–1904), 3:379–80. For Chaucer and the daisy poetry, see Lowes, "The Prologue to the *LGW* as Related to the French Marguerite Poems."

daisy and the daisies of his French contemporaries: Chaucer's flower does not have any direct and obvious affiliation with a real woman—or even a fictional woman of the courtly variety. Instead, she is associated with a classical figure, whose legend Chaucer would have come to know from books. Moreover, the existence of the *marguerite* tradition (as well as the closely allied "flower and leaf" debates mentioned in the *Legend*'s Prologue) cannot stand as the sole reason for Chaucer's writing of the *Legend*, for he himself makes it clear that his poem is "of another tonne" (F 195, G 79).[9] Thus continental daisy poetry, though providing an important literary precedent for Chaucer's Alceste, does not go far enough in explaining the identity of this "lady sovereyne."

Critics of the *Legend* have also noted that in addition to her identity as a daisy, Alceste seems to be related to Venus, in part because her fellowship with the God of Love suggests a shared authority over the amatory realm described in the Prologue. And if one views her in yet another light, she resembles the Virgin Mary in her intercessory role, made necessary by the ire of the angry deity she accompanies.[10] But in our attempts to keep Alceste thoroughly medieval, we must not forget that she is also the Alcestis of Greek and Roman mythology. The reasons behind Chaucer's decision to employ the relatively obscure Alcestis legend have yet to be cogently explained. This book will explore the connections this legend has to Chaucer's interest in describing and defending his own principles of retelling classical tales.

Like all effective figures in allegorical poetry, Alceste and the God of Love are to some extent multivalent, that is, they exist within more than one sphere of meaning.[11] Although they

[9]All line references to Chaucer's works are from the second edition of F. N. Robinson (Boston: Houghton Mifflin, 1957).

[10]See Payne, *Key of Remembrance*, p. 107, for a discussion of Alceste as Venus. She is probably not intended to be identified with this goddess, however, because the God of Love refers to Venus as if she were not there (F 338, G 313). On Alceste as an intercessor, see Payne, pp. 107–8.

[11]On allegory's ability to convey multiple meanings, see, for example, Michael Murrin, *The Veil of Allegory* (Chicago: Univ. of Chicago Press, 1969), pp. 101–5; Gay Clifford, *The Transformations of Allegory* (London: Routledge and

straightforwardly and dramatically announce their views on literature, on the "good women" of antiquity, and on Chaucer's former works, they also indirectly represent certain larger concepts that Chaucer wanted to convey, and it is only with these concepts in mind that this poem's dialogue can be properly understood. That is, Alceste and the God of Love participate not only in a literal action but also in an allegorical one that provides information beyond what their literal words and actions express. The great complexity of these two allegorical characters makes the task of reading (and writing about) the *Legend* a difficult one, for it requires constant attention to two separate, though related, levels of meaning.

Understanding the Prologue, however, is only the first step toward understanding the *Legend* as a whole. The stories that make up the legendary proper, classical in subject matter and in some instances closely translated from Latin sources, have not been studied adequately in terms of their relationship to one another or to the Prologue that introduces them. There are, I fear, legions of unsatisfied readers of these stories, most of whom think them narrative failures, understandably abandoned by the poet himself.[12] Even Robert Worth Frank, whose book on the *Legend* attempts a vindication of the bravest sort, admits that there are lapses of proper emphasis and selection in some of the stories.[13] Whether we view them as true failures or as parodies, like the stories in the *Monk's Tale*, of the kinds of narratives Chaucer himself considered failures, we must still decide what the poet intended when he composed them. Most problematic of all, perhaps, is the rubric under which the stories are written—the legendary itself. Why Chaucer chose the

Kegan Paul, 1974), pp. 50–53, 95–97; Angus Fletcher, *Allegory: The Theory of a Symbolic Mode* (Ithaca, N.Y.: Cornell Univ. Press, 1964), pp. 220–36; Rosamund Tuve, *Allegorical Imagery* (Princeton, N.J.: Princeton Univ. Press, 1966), pp. 199, 328, 330; Paul Piehler, *The Visionary Landscape: A Study in Medieval Allegory* (London: Edward Arnold, 1971), pp. 11, 14; and Maureen Quilligan, *The Language of Allegory: Defining the Genre* (Ithaca, N.Y.: Cornell Univ. Press, 1979), pp. 33–40.
[12]For a summary of these critical views, see Frank, pp. 189–210.
[13]Frank, p. 172.

saint's life as a paradigm for his classical stories is a question whose answer is essential to any conclusive interpretation of the poem as a whole. To what extent we are to ignore the suicidal tendencies of these classical ladies or to conceive of their suicide and despair as forms of Christian martyrdom is difficult to determine, but it is an issue that must be confronted by any responsible critic of the *Legend of Good Women*.

Alceste, the God of Love, and the stories they inspire all need substantial critical attention, not only in terms of the poem that contains them, but also in terms of the fourteenth-century culture in which their origins ultimately lie. Robert O. Payne, one of the *Legend's* best critics, was the first to draw attention to the importance of this poem, noting that it displayed Chaucer's mature interest in the synthesis of experience, vision, and tradition in a poet's invention of subject matter.[14] But the poem is also about something more specific. It is, above all, about the survival of classical fiction in a Christian world. In the *Legend*, the narrator is the bearer of the "key of remembrance"; he is a teller of classical tales in a poem about the preservation and dissemination, through literature, of classical wisdom. The *Legend* is also a poem about the difficulties inherent in Chaucer's role as a teller of others' tales, one who has obligations to his sources and also to the new and different audience for whom these sources were to be adapted.

To present his views on the uses of classical fiction, Chaucer finds it necessary to include several other serious issues in his poem as well. He reacts to certain traditional theories of art, he comments on allegorization (one of the commonest ways in which medieval poets made classical texts confirm Christian truth), he reveals to us many fourteenth-century assumptions about literature's usefulness to everyday life, and he betrays his beliefs about the act and purpose of translation. Once we have fully appreciated the richness of this poem, we are forced to realize once again what we have known previously about Chaucer's love poetry: that it serves as an ample vehicle for all

---

[14]*Key of Remembrance*, pp. 100–101.

kinds of subjects, not only the amatory ones it overtly concerns. And even though the *Legend* seems less "complete" than Chaucer's greatest unfinished collection of stories, the *Canterbury Tales*, it is surely one of the most ambitious of his mature works, for in the *Legend* Chaucer sets forth the fundamental principles behind his use of "olde thynges"—the very principles that allowed him, in all his works, to convey so successfully the wisdom of his classical masters in his own distinctive voice.

— 1 —

Daisies, the Sun,
and Poetry

Recently Chaucerians have attempted to relate the poet's works to their thirteenth- and fourteenth-century philosophical contexts. In books and articles about Chaucer published in recent years, we frequently encounter the names of William of Ockham, Roger Bacon, and John Duns Scotus, and we find literary scholars applying terms such as "nominalism," "realism," "accidents," and "universals" to Chaucer's works. Similarly, fourteenth-century philosophical trends have been discovered and analyzed, resulting in the now widely acknowledged belief that Chaucer and his contemporaries lived in an age that began to approve of empiricism as a foundation for epistemological inquiry and that earlier tendencies to seek universal a priori patterns in the world were giving way to make room for serious investigations into the particularity of things.[1] Critics of Chaucer have also suggested that along with the realization that the

[1]For a general discussion of Ockham, nominalism, and the individuation of experience, see Gordon Leff, *Medieval Thought: Augustine to Ockham* (Baltimore: Penguin Books, 1958), pp. 259–84, David Knowles, *The Evolution of Medieval Thought* (New York: Random House, 1962), pp. 311–36, and F. C. Copleston, *A History of Medieval Philosophy* (New York: Harper and Row, 1972), pp. 230–56. For discussion of these trends in Chaucer's works, see, for example, Robert Burlin, *Chaucerian Fiction* (Princeton, N.J.: Princeton Univ. Press, 1977), pp. 3–22, and Sheila Delany, *Chaucer's House of Fame: The Poetics of Skeptical Fideism* (Chicago: Univ. of Chicago Press, 1972), pp. 7–21.

world was comprised of individual facts, which taken together provided a valid basis for deriving knowledge, came an interest among fourteenth-century artists in weighing the relative merits of "experience" and "authority" as sources for literary works, a dichotomy Chaucer himself acknowledges in the opening lines of the Wife of Bath's Prologue and in the *Legend*'s preliminary remarks.

Unfortunately, it is impossible for us to know how much contact Chaucer had with the philosophical *via moderna* which was being paved at Oxford in the late fourteenth century, and, lamentably, we do not have the writings of the "philosophical Strode" to aid us in our understanding of these and other issues. In spite of what we think we know about fourteenth-century philosophy, its subtle and intricate geography is still, in large part, uncharted. We can probably state with certainty, however, that Chaucer never took sides in any raging debate between the thinkers who favored authority as a means of acquiring knowledge and those who believed that experience was the best resource to tap in the search for truth. No debate like this is likely ever to have occurred between two such clearly defined camps. But evident in Chaucer's works is the realization that these two sources of knowledge are often in conflict with one another and just as often do not allow any resolution in the form of easy syntheses. In the Wife of Bath, for example, we see a woman who structures her thought by means of this dialectic and who is consequently condemned, it appears, to endless travel between its extremes. However, she is not wrong to question authority by contradicting it with her experience, nor is she wrong to seek authorities that confirm for her the morality of her rather disordered life. The restless vacillation and radical uncertainty that plague this woman's intellectual state are not merely comic traits; she has, after all, reduced to the terms of everyday life the problems that plague us all. Chaucer wrote sympathetically about her because even for Chaucer the artist (let alone Chaucer in his other roles) the problem of experience and authority affected him considerably, defining, as it did, the very essence of his art. Though he realized the lasting value of authoritative statements made by poets of the past, he, like all artists, also wanted to make his poetry speak with the voice of experiential truth.

The *Legend of Good Women* confronts this problem in significant ways, made manifest in the opening lines of the Prologue, which set forth the theme as clearly as Chaucer ever saw fit to do:

> A thousand tymes have I herd men telle
> That ther ys joy in hevene and peyne in helle,
> And I acorde wel that it ys so;
> But, natheles, yet wot I wel also
> That ther nis noon dwellyng in this contree,
> That eyther hath in hevene or helle ybe,
> Ne may of hit noon other weyes witen,
> But as he hath herd seyd, or founde it writen;
> For by assay ther may no man it preve.
> But God forbede but men shulde leve
> Wel more thing then men han seen with ye!
> Men shal not wenen every thing a lye
> But yf himself yt seeth, or elles dooth;
> For, God wot, thing is never the lasse sooth,
> Thogh every wight ne may it nat ysee.
> [F, G 1–15]

Justly famous for their defense of written culture, these lines argue that truth must be learned from written accounts as well as from experience, and people must not, in any newly sanctioned quest for "preve," forget the information that books can offer them, especially those books whose subject matter extends beyond their own experience. "Wel ought us thanne honouren and beleve/These bokes, there we han noon other preve" (F, G 27–28), Chaucer concludes, realizing that there exist many things that people will never see for themselves, things that can be known only through the "doctrine of these olde wyse" (F, G 19) as it is discovered in books. Even "Bernard the monk," whose monastic experience was supposedly richly enhanced by several actual visits from the Word, "ne saugh nat all, pardee!" (F, G 16).[2]

Heaven and hell—to use Chaucer's extreme cases—are, of course, alien to the experience of all of us "dwellyng in this contree," so our knowledge of these places must depend on someone else's accounts of what exists there. But the same is true even for our knowledge of certain natural phenomena; the study of astronomy, for example, is beyond the capabilities of most earth-bound scholars, who do not often get the opportunity to journey through the skies with a learned eagle, as does "Geffrey" in the *House of Fame*. But even the lucky Geffrey, it seems, is on that celestial journey against his will, for he knows perfectly well that he can sit at home and read about the constellations rather than be exposed to the considerable risks involved in actually seeing them. In response to the eagle's insistence that he look around him, he says:

> "No fors," quod y, "hyt is no nede.
> I leve as wel, so God me spede,
> Hem that write of this matere,
> As though I knew her places here. . . ."
>
> [1011–14]

In fact, the light emitted by the stars burns our narrator's eyes, indicating that in this case at least, direct experience is harmful to man's weak faculties:

> "And eke they shynen here so bryghte
> Hyt shulde shenden al my syghte
> To loke on hem."[3]
>
> [1015–17]

[2]In this context, it is appropriate to identify "Bernard the monk" as Bernard of Clairvaux because he claimed to have had direct personal experience of God. As M. Corneille Haflants writes: "In the course of the Sermons Bernard frequently appeals to his own experience. His whole life and doctrine were illumined by the mystic visits of the Word with which he confesses to have been blest. It is these personal contacts with God which made him so great a saint." Haflants is writing in *On the Song of Songs I, The Works of Bernard of Clairvaux*, vol. 2, Cistercian Fathers Series, no. 4 (Spencer, Mass.: Cistercian Publications, 1971), p. x.

[3]On the bright stars that celestial travelers find difficult to endure, see Alain de Lille's *Anticlaudianus*, trans. James J. Sheridan (Toronto: Pontifical Institute

These remarks show that Geffrey knows he can both save his vision and learn about the stars by reading books by "hem that write of this matere."[4] That is, through literature's vicarious encounters and through the indirect "vision" that books afford, people can "observe" the stars, their light, heaven, hell, and any other distant or even physically intolerable phenomena they may wish to investigate.

Chaucer's involvement with this theme is also evident in *Troilus and Criseyde*, which, like the *House of Fame*, predates the introductory lines of the *Legend* quoted above in which the poet takes his strongest stand on the validity of written culture. In Book 2, Antigone sings a song in praise of love which seems to contradict Chaucer's views on the limitations of experience and which bears a very important relationship to the *Legend*. She claims that all criticism of love originates in ignorance, since those who disparage it have evidently never experienced the perfect bliss, joy, and security it offers. Among the several analogies she uses to elucidate her point, she includes the following, in which she notes that the sun is no less worthy just because human vision cannot tolerate its brightness:

> "What is the sonne wers, of kynde right,
> Though that a man, for feeblesse of his yen,
> May nought endure on it to see for bright?"
>
> [862–64]

And after her song is finished, Antigone, with a curiously impractical suggestion, tells Criseyde that people in search of any kind of knowledge about love must first experience it. After all,

---

of Mediaeval Studies, 1973): "Here man's faltering steps would stray from the path: even his feet would wander drunkenly and sight, that lights the feet, would grow dull and inactive and refuse its guidance, and the eye, faced with the light there would prove sightless" (5.50–54). Also see Alain's description of Lady Astronomy: "Bright light gleams on her face and when lightning flashes from it, it strikes our gazing eyes, and shunning the full-blown lightning, they fear to open their lids" (4.8–10).

[4]Chaucer may be thinking here of great cosmological poems such as Martianus Capella's *De nuptiis philologiae et mercurii*, Bernard Silvester's *Cosmographia*, and Alain de Lille's *Anticlaudianus*.

she concludes, no one knows about the fairness of heaven better than saints who have been there, and no one can describe the foulness of hell better than its resident fiends (2.894–96).

To be sure, experience may be the best of all teachers, as perhaps Troilus himself is destined to find out, but Chaucer is not willing to restrict the range of human knowledge to what experience alone can teach. Antigone's point of view is much too extreme to be shared by Chaucer, at least at the time he wrote the *Legend*'s opening lines. We should not, writes the poet, judge things to be untrue just because we have not validated them by our own personal experience; our eyesight is weak, our experience is limited, and our visits to heaven and hell are few and far between. The *Troilus* itself stands to teach us this truth: even though Troilus's experiences are not our own, we the readers of his story come to know something of love's joys and pains, and we never doubt that the knowledge we receive from reading Chaucer's poem is useful, adequate, and true. Knowledge through literature, though perhaps not a substitute for what can be learned through the immediacy and the involvement of experience, is nonetheless a valid kind of knowledge—and one that we depend upon. Moreover, as Antigone's sun analogy suggests, in some cases experience can be too intense, just as the light of the sun is unendurable to human eyes. But Chaucer addresses this particular problem, too: only six stanzas after Antigone's reference to the sun, he demonstrates how he, as a poet, can provide his readers with a glimpse of the sun's blinding light, a glimpse that does not jeopardize vision. With three short but descriptive figures, Chaucer describes the sun, offering his readers a clever example of how poets make possible a kind of "indirect vision," one that has its basis in metaphor:

> The dayes honour, and the hevenes yë,
> The nyghtes foo—al this clepe I the sonne. . . .
> [2.904–5]

The bright stars in the *House of Fame* and the metaphorical "solution" to the problem raised in Antigone's sun analogy both serve to adumbrate the *Legend*'s opening issue, that is, the importance of literature as a preserver and conveyor of knowledge, especially the kind of knowledge that cannot otherwise be gained. In the debate that Chaucer alludes to in the *Legend*'s opening remarks, he is clearly taking the stand that "authority" has a defensible—indeed necessary—role in human epistemology.

As further corroboration of Chaucer's faith in the efficacy of literary alternatives to direct experience, we need only remember that Chaucer the love poet constantly claims, in the voice of his persona, that he himself never experienced the joys or pains of love. Throughout his career as a poet, Chaucer acknowledges (sometimes humorously) that he is not himself a lover but instead a mere reporter, lurking on the fringes of the amatory world in order to record for posterity others' pains and joys. But even though he claims never to have known personal service under Love's hard laws (in the *Troilus*, he is a "servant of the servants of love"), he manages to record his stories about lovers with engagement and sympathy. In other words, Chaucer's claims of personal distance from the experience itself never prevented him from becoming an expert on love and its risks, for Chaucer was a competent love poet more than anything else—one who wrote convincingly all his life about love's effects on human destiny. His reputed lack of experience in love in no way affected the extent or power of his observations about it. Chaucer tells us in a few of the *Legend*'s early lines how his expertise was possible: he learned about love from reading the works of the classical and medieval love poets before him, those who had "of makyng ropen, and lad awey the corn" (F 74, G 62). Chaucer's reading, then, followed by his own "rehearsing" of material gleaned from the poets of the past, first informed him about the subject of love and then ensured the survival and dissemination of these amatory truths, even in the absence of experiential facts. Chaucer, like all artists, counts among literature's many gifts its ability to protect us from life's misfortunes while allowing us a clear vision of such tragedies by lending them an artistic form that cannot harm us.

As the quotations from the *House of Fame* and the *Troilus* show, certain kinds of direct experience are intolerable; for these we can effectively substitute the much less extreme source of knowledge, literature, which can expose us to suns that in reality might blind.

In his dream, the narrator of the *Legend* is given a kind of amatory beatific vision (perhaps meant to be the amatory equivalent of Bernard's spiritual meetings with God) which includes a confrontation with a personified version of love itself, the very state that Chaucer claims to have avoided all his life. This comic character is an imperious figure, as we might expect a deity to be, and he displays attributes of the Christian God, as do the similar deities in French and Italian amatory verse. In keeping with Chaucer's feelings on the terrifying nature of direct experience, the God of Love is formidable indeed, with his fiery arrows and his menacing looks. But the God of Love's most striking feature is his bright face, which in both versions of the *Legend*'s Prologue shines with a brilliance that nearly blinds the narrator:

> His gilte heer was corowned with a sonne,
> Instede of gold, for hevynesse and wyghte.
> Therwith me thoghte his face shoon so bryghte
> That wel unnethes myghte I him beholde.
>
> [F 230–33]

In the G text, we find a similar description:

> But of his face I can not seyn the hewe;
> For sikerly his face shon so bryghte
> That with the glem astoned was the syghte;
> A furlong-wey I myhte hym not behold.
>
> [G 162–65]

Introduced in this way, the God of Love carries with him not only Chaucer's comical statement on the extreme nature of direct experience (cast in the same terms used in the *House of Fame*) but also a rich store of traditional connotations that classical and medieval writers, beginning with Plato, associated with the sun. The most important of these connotations is the sun's identification with truth—and ultimately God. Poets and theologians had for centuries compared the light of truth (both secular and divine) to the light of the sun. Among theologians alone, the analogy had been used from the third century, in the works of the Christian apologist Minucius Felix, to well beyond Chaucer's own lifetime.[5] Dante, to name but one important writer who gave expression to this idea, found "no sensible thing in the entire world . . . more deserving of being made a type of God than the sun," for it illuminates all elements with

---

[5]Students of Dante, of course, have proven to be the best researchers of this subject. See especially Joseph Anthony Mazzeo, *Medieval Cultural Tradition in Dante's Comedy* (Ithaca, N.Y.: Cornell Univ. Press, 1960), pp. 56–132; Allan H. Gilbert, *Dante and His Comedy* (New York: New York Univ. Press, 1963), pp. 7–17; Charles S. Singleton, *Journey to Beatrice*, Dante Studies, 2 (Cambridge, Mass.: Harvard Univ. Press, 1958), pp. 15–34; and Marcia Colish, *The Mirror of Language* (New Haven, Conn.: Yale Univ. Press, 1968), pp. 253, 332. The most extensive treatment of the sun in medieval literature occurs in H. Flanders Dunbar's *Symbolism in Medieval Thought and Its Consummation in the Divine Comedy* (New Haven, Conn.: Yale Univ. Press, 1929), pp. 105–229, in which Dunbar cites two helpful references. The first is a quotation by the early Christian apologist Minucius Felix: ". . . we cannot even look into the sun, which is the origin of vision; our powers of sight are impaired by its rays, our eyes are weakened by gazing at it, and if we look at it too long, we are unable to see at all. . . . Do you expect to look upon God with the eyes of flesh?" (p. 133). The second concerns Rabanus Maurus, who "made a catalogue in which he adduced scriptural passages to show that the sun symbolizes *Deus, resurrectio Christi, Sancta Ecclesia,* . . . etc." (p. 274). Other medieval examples of the notion of bright divinity occur in the medieval cycle plays. The *Ludus Coventriae*, a source closer to Chaucer in time and sensibility than the passages quoted above, shows that a midwife present at the Nativity is stunned by the light that emanates from the manger: "Me merveylyth wyff surely your face I can not se/but as þe sonne with his bemys·quan he is most bryth" (K. S. Block, ed., EETS e.s. 120 [London, 1922], p. 109). That the sun analogy pertained to the investigations of theologians, see Dante's Circle of the Sun, *Paradiso* 10. That it pertained to the "multifoliate rose" of the saints and angels, see *Paradiso* 30–33. On the medieval aesthetics of light, see Edgar De Bruyne, *The Esthetics of the Middle Ages,* trans. Eileen B. Hennessy (New York: Frederick Ungar, 1969), pp. 16–18, 55–61. Finally, the thirteenth-century optician and philosopher John of Pecham writes in his *Perspectiva communis* that "the action of bright lights on the eyes is sensibly painful and injurious . . . but the sight is strengthened and amplified by rays that are obliquely incident on the eye" (David L. Lindberg, ed. and trans., *John of Pecham and the Science of Optics* [Madison: Univ. of Wisconsin Press, 1970], pp. 125–27).

sensible light and all intelligible creatures with light for the intellect.[6] The sun analogy is important to Chaucer's *Legend* because it describes a Christian epistemological paradox that relates to the work that poets do. The paradox is this: despite people's dependence on truth, for one reason or another they are usually unfit to receive it. Using the sun analogy, Christian theologians cast the problem into these terms: either a person is unable to see truth's light at all because of the clouded vision characteristic of his fallen state, or, when finally confronted with the light in all its unalloyed splendor, he is unable to look directly upon it with unaided eyes, much as he is unable to gaze upon the sun. Augustine, for example, supplies us with one use of this analogy in *De doctrina Christiana*, where he writes about the epistemological shortcomings caused by human sinfulness. Knowledge of God is impossible, he states, until the eye of the mind is cleansed of its impurities, for the Trinity glows with a light that contaminated eyes cannot tolerate.[7] Yet in spite of the brilliant intensity of God's light, theologians and philosophers continued to urge man to attempt to find it—and then gaze upon it. Boethius's Lady Philosophy hopes to teach her charge about dispelling the dark "mists" that distort his vision, for instance; then, (as Chaucer translates) "schyneth Phebus ischaken with sodeyn light, and smyteth with his beemes in merveylynge eien."[8] Continuing the analogy, she states:

> That derknesse schal I assaie somwhat to maken thynne and wayk by lyghte and meneliche remedies; so that, aftir that the derknesse of desceyvynge desyrynges is doon away, thow mowe knowe the schynynge of verray light.
>
> [*Boece* 1, Prose 6]

---

[6]*Convivio* 3.12.6–7, trans. Robert S. Haller, in *Literary Criticism of Dante Alighieri* (Lincoln: Univ. of Nebraska Press, 1973), p. 120.

[7]*De doctrina Christiana* 2.7.11 (D. W. Robertson, Jr., trans., *On Christian Doctrine* [Indianapolis: Bobbs-Merrill, 1958], p. 39). Augustine also writes that after our eyes are purified, "the light of the Trinity begins to appear more certainly, and not only more tolerably but also more joyfully . . . [but] it is still said to appear 'through a glass in a dark manner'" (2.7.11, p. 40).

[8]*Boece* 1, Met. 3.

Even Chaucer's own Parson finds the sun analogy useful in his humble moral text; he tells us that "'the derknesse of deeth' been the synnes that the wrecched man hath doon, whiche that destourben hym to see the face of God, right as dooth a derk clowde bitwixe us and the sonne."[9] But sinfulness and the natural human tendency to absorb oneself in worldly affairs are not the only reasons for one's inability to perceive the divine truths of heaven. God himself prevented direct perception of his light, in part by investing his creation (the world and the Bible both) with allegorical obscurity, such as that which Augustine writes about in this passage on expounding a difficult Scriptural truth:

> He has covered His light with clouds beneath, and it is difficult to fly, eagle-like, above every mist with which all the earth is covered, and to see in the words of the Lord most unalloyed light. In case He may scatter asunder our darkness with the warmth of His rays and afterwards open Himself to us, let us defer these questions.[10]

Gregory, too, described Scriptural truth in these terms; he writes that it is an "image of the sun as seen through a cloud or mist."[11] Indeed all through the Middle Ages, the analogy of the sun and clouds, perhaps given authority by Augustine's doctrine of divine illumination, was considered an accurate representation of how humans understand divine matters. In particular, the writings of the late medieval mystics show a thorough appropriation of this analogy because the conservative brand of spirituality in which they believed depended upon the survival of the epistemological theory that the sun analogy expressed.[12]

Recognition of the sun analogy's importance to medieval

[9]*Parson's Tale*, 184.
[10]*Homilies on the Gospel according to St. John* (Oxford: Parker, 1848), vol. 1 sec. 5.22–23. Translated by Dunbar in *Symbolism in Medieval Thought*, p. 149. I have slightly modernized the translation.
[11]Gregory's formulation is mentioned in Dunbar, p. 151. Dunbar dates Gregory as the first to use this image as a description of biblical allegory.
[12]See, for example, *The Cloud of Unknowing*. Also see *Qui Habitat*, by the fourteenth-century Pseudo–Walter Hilton, in *An Exposition of Qui Habitat and*

thought may not at first seem crucial to an understanding of Chaucer's satiric God of Love. But the relationship between the sun analogy and the *Legend*'s issues becomes much clearer when we see how this essentially theological model was adopted by theorists of art to describe—and finally justify—art's function in the Christian world. It is well worth our effort to explore the extension of the sun analogy into medieval literary discourse in particular, for it is from this tradition that Chaucer derives one of the basic assumptions informing the *Legend*'s Prologue. Even outside the circles of the parsons and mystics, the sun analogy had been viewed as having explanatory power, especially as it conveyed the terms of symbolic theory. Since genuine beatific vision—including, of course, any direct revelation of divine truth to humanity—was considered possible for only a chosen few, the human majority was dependent upon the already existing symbolic representations of God's truths, the two most important of which were considered to be Scripture and the created world. And once the example of Scripture's allegorical representation of truth had been fully absorbed into Christian thought (as in the formulations of Augustine and Gregory given above), it did not take long for the model to be secularized and consequently pressed into service as a defense of literary representation in general.

For the Middle Ages, one of the most authoritative defenders of the symbolic mode—and finally art in all its representational functions—was Macrobius, who, in his commentary on Cicero's *Somnium Scipionis*, refers to the necessary functions of certain literary devices. About philosophers he writes:

> When they wish to assign attributes to these divinities that not only pass the bounds of speech but those of human comprehen-

---

Bonum Est, ed. Björn Wallner, Lund Studies in English 23 (Lund, 1954), where the author writes that the light of the midday fiend "shineþ alwey bi-twene two blake cloudes; þat on is heiȝnesse of himself þorw presumpcion, colourd under fredam of spirit, and þat oþur is a-douncastyng of his even-cristen undurneþe him. . . . But þese cloudes vanisscheþ a-wei whon þe liht of grace scheweþ"(pp. 22–23). For the survival of orthodox thought in mystical writings, see Copleston, *A History of Medieval Philosophy*, pp. 277–91.

sion as well, they resort to similes and analogies. That is why Plato, when he was moved to speak about the Good, did not dare to tell what it was, knowing only this about it, that it was impossible for the human mind to grasp what it was. In truth, of visible objects he found the sun most like it, and by using this as an illustration opened a way for his discourse to approach what was otherwise incomprehensible.[13]

Here the heuristic value of analogy and simile, which consists of their effectiveness in illustrating truth for insufficient human perceptions, is paired with Plato's own use of the sun as an image of the Good, a connection that certainly helped the sun analogy move as swiftly as it did into medieval theories of literary meaning. The twelfth-century humanists, interested in discovering Christian uses for pagan literature, also had much to do with the extension of this analogy into general poetic theory; it occurs repeatedly in their own poems and in their writings on the functions of philosophy and literature.[14] And Dante, the greatest of the poet-theologians, chooses this analogy as the paradigm of his career; in a sense, his works trace the story of an individual striving, with the help of the mediation provided by symbolic forms, to view the injurious but lifegiving rays of God.

It is really this last idea—that art mediates between the "mind's eye" and the "bright object" it seeks to contemplate—that engaged the thoughts of medieval poets and schol-

---

[13]Macrobius's *Commentary on the Dream of Scipio*, trans. William Harris Stahl (New York: Columbia Univ. Press, 1952), p. 86.

[14]For example, Winthrop Wetherbee, in his translation of Bernard Silvester's *Cosmographia*, notes a connection between the dazzling light given off by the sunlike Tugaton and Plato's "Good" (Wetherbee, trans., *The Cosmographia of Bernardus Silvestris* [New York: Columbia Univ. Press, 1973], p. 158n. Tugaton's radiance is "inaccessible" and confounds the vision of the beholder (Wetherbee, p. 99). The description of this "triune radiance" recalls, as Wetherbee notes, the account of the procession of the Word in pseudo-Dionysius's *On Celestial Hierarchy*, which was translated by John Scotus Erigena. See also the *Anticlaudianus* of Alain de Lille, in which Faith gives Prudence a mirror to interpose between her eyes and the injurious light from the sunlike God (6.115–35).

ars. Boccaccio, when he wished to explain the difficulty of classical narratives, employed this concept to account for the
hidden meanings of myth. In his *Genealogia deorum gentilium*, he
writes:

> Some things are naturally so profound that not without difficulty
> can the most exceptional keenness in intellect sound their depths;
> like the sun's globe, by which, before they can clearly discern it,
> strong eyes are sometimes repelled. On the other hand, some
> things, though naturally clear perhaps, are so veiled by the artist's
> skill that scarcely anyone could by mental effort derive sense from
> them; as the immense body of the sun when hidden in clouds
> cannot be exactly located by the eye of the most learned astrono-
> mer.[15]

Petrarch agrees:

> . . . poets under the veil of fictions have set forth truths physical,
> moral, and historical—thus bearing out a statement I often make,
> that the difference between a poet on the one hand and a histo-
> rian or a moral or physical philosopher on the other is the same as
> the difference between a clouded sky and a clear sky, since in
> each case the same light exists in the object of vision, but is per-
> ceived in different degrees according to the capacity of the
> observers.[16]

In other words, though poetry's obliquity may reduce the intensity of bright truths, it by no means decreases the amount of
"light" available to its readers. Such a convincing defense of
poetry's method did not die out with the medieval period; by
Spenser's time, it was still central—sun and all—to the allegorical writers. In Book 2 of *The Faerie Queene*, Spenser writes that
the character of his Princess will be presented obliquely,

[15]Book 14.12 This translation is by Charles G. Osgood in *Boccaccio on Poetry*
(Indianapolis: Bobbs-Merrill, 1956), p. 59.
[16]This passage is translated by E. H. Wilkins, "Petrarch's Coronation Oration," *PMLA*, 68 (1953), 1246.

> . . . thus to enfold
> In covert vele, and wrap in shadowes light,
> That feeble eyes your glory may behold,
> Which else could not endure those beames bright
> But would be dazzled with exceeding light.[17]

[2.5]

The "clouded sky" of Boccaccio and Petrarch, and the "covert vele" and "shadowes light" of Spenser are all versions of the single sun analogy by which medieval poets attempted to describe the function and necessity of literature's indirectness. And now, returning to Chaucer, we are able to clarify one of the *Legend*'s major structural obscurities, namely, how the dazzling God of Love relates to the *Legend*'s opening lines on the value of literary truth. The necessity for some kind of indirect representation, some alternative yet legitimate form of truth to replace the narrator's immediate experience of love is given Christian authority (by Chaucer's appropriation of the sun analogy) and dramatic "proof" in this little springtime dream. The awesome intensity of Love's sunlike visage is too much for our dazzled narrator; he requires an intercessor to diminish the intensity of Love's bright light yet to preserve for him the essential lessons that this visit from Love might offer. The intercessor in this analogical scheme, the one who lessens light yet conveys its truth, is Alceste, the chief provider of comfort for the Prologue's timid narrator and a symbol of literature's mediating role.

The first time we meet Alceste, she is introduced in terms that define her as an intercessor between the narrator and the God of Love's words and "chere":

> For, nadde comfort ben of hire presence,
> I hadde ben ded, withouten any defence,

[17]*Poetical Works*, ed. J. C. Smith and E. de Selincourt (Oxford: Oxford Univ. Press, 1970). See also Murrin, p. 17, where the author quotes from (but does not comment upon) Harrington: "Therefore we do first read some other authors, making them as it were a looking-glass to the eyes of our minde, and then after we have gathered more strength, we enter into profounder studies

For drede of Loves wordes and his chere,
As, when tyme ys, herafter ye shal here.
[F 278–81, G 181–84]

To be sure, Alceste intercedes quite vociferously on the narrator's behalf later in the *Legend*'s Prologue when she defends
him from charges of literary crime. In that sense, she protects
Chaucer from the threat of "Loves wordes." But the other intercessory role she plays, before a word is spoken about Chaucer's former art, is much more essential to the Prologue's
scheme. By interceding between light and the human vision for
which that light is intended, Alceste dramatizes what Chaucer
claims to be literature's most defensible function: its ability to
offer an alternative to direct perception. To explain how and
why Alceste functions as the "poetic veil" that stands between
readers and truth we must first examine the daisy from which
she is constructed.

Before the narrator's dream begins, we are given an elaborate and seemingly digressive account of the habits and attributes of Chaucer's "lady sovereyne," his daisy. Far from being
trivial, however, these descriptive passages tell us exactly what
there is about the daisy that makes it a fitting model for poetry's symbolic method, specifically the kind of poetry Chaucer
himself chose to produce. All through the Prologue's early sections, in deceptively simple phrases that imitate the empty plati-
tudes of courtly love verse, Chaucer slyly lets us know of the
"poetic" possibilities of his lady the daisy. She is the mistress of
his wit (F 88), "of alle floures flour" (F 53, G 55)—one thinks
here of the flowers of rhetoric—the "erthly god" that serves as
Muse for Chaucer, "bothe in this werk and in my sorwes alle"
(F 95–96), and the lady who best serves to inspire his verse:
"My word, my werk ys knyt . . . in youre bond" (F 89). But the
most significant attribute of Chaucer's flower is its relationship
to the sun, that relationship which best defines its purpose in
this Prologue. As with any flower in the natural world, the

_of high mysteries, having first as it were enabled our eyes by long beholdinge
the sunne in a bason of water at last to looke upon the sunne itself."_

—43—

poet's daisy cannot exist without the life-giving rays of the sun. The flower even rises and sets in close imitation of the rising and setting sun:

> As I seyde erst, whanne comen is the May,
> That in my bed ther daweth me no day
> That I nam up and walkyng in the mede
> To seen this flour ayein the sonne sprede,
> Whan it upryseth erly by the morwe.
>
> [F 45–49, G 45–49]

As long as the sun shines, the daisy remains open, with its petals "sprad in the brightnesse/Of the sonne" (F 64–65) to catch its rays of light. But as darkness approaches, it begins to close:

> And whan that hit ys eve, I renne blyve,
> As sone as evere the sonne gynneth weste,
> To seen this flour, how it wol go to reste,
> For fere of nyght, so hateth she derknesse.
>
> [F 60–63]

Chaucer is not unique in noting the daisy's relationship to the sun.[18] Its heliotropism and fear of night are mentioned in several of the French *marguerite* poems, which Chaucer had surely read before beginning the *Legend*. His eagerness to be present at the daisy's "resureccioun," to watch it "whan that yt shulde unclose/Agayn the sonne" (F 110–12) is also characteristic of several of the French narrators.[19] But in Chaucer's poem, where the daisy stands as a model for his art, the sun, which gives this flower its life, represents something that informs and sustains his verse. Just as all flowers depend for their lives on the light of the sun, so all poets, even the worst of them, define their verse as drawing energy from the light of truth. Thus the

---

[18]The daisy's heliotropism is mentioned in Machaut, *Dit de la Marguerite*, in *Oeuvres*, p. 123; *Dit de la fleur de lis et de la Marguerite*, in *Marguerite Poetry*, ed. Wimsatt, ll. 251–58; Deschamps, *Lai de Franchise*, in *Oeuvres* 2:203–14, ll. 40–52, Froissart, *Dittié de la flour de la Margherite*, in *Oeuvres* 2:211, ll. 53–62; 2:214, ll. 162–66.

[19]See Wimsatt, p. 33.

flower's dependence on light is here seen as analogous to poetry's dependence on the truth that guides and sustains it.

Still another attribute of the daisy that makes it a fitting
model for poetry involves its natural resemblance to the sun.
Just as poetry imitates truth, so the daisy imitates the sun in
both shape and color, having raylike yellow or white petals that
surround a bright center. And in order to extend even further
his daisy's physical likeness to the sun, Chaucer endows his
flower with a clear and guiding light, drawing more terminology from the world of courtly love:

> She is the clernesse and the verray lyght
> That in this derke world me wynt and ledeth.
>
> [F 84–85]

Chaucer's daisy, then, is an earthly imitation of the sun. Its
physical form is closer to the sun's than to any other natural object's, and its light is clear and true, able to guide men through
the dark world. Affording illumination without blinding intensity, the daisy, like poetry, conveys the light of heaven in a
manner suitable for earthly eyes.

But perhaps Chaucer's most important reason for choosing
the daisy over all other flowers to remind us of poetry lies in
the name of the flower itself. Philologists and critics have remarked with delight that the poet's description of the daisy in
the Prologue contains something rare and surprising for a medieval work—a true etymology:

> The longe day I shoop me for t'abide
> For nothing elles, and I shal nat lye,
> But for to loke upon the dayesie,
> That wel by reson men it calle may
> The "dayesye," or elles the "ye of day." . . .
>
> [F 180–84]

Indeed, by modern philological standards, Chaucer's deriva-
tion is perfectly sound; he has analyzed the word by recording

both its form and its meaning from an earlier stage of the language. But the study of etymology in medieval times was, of course, much different from what it is today. Etymologies, both true and fictional, were seen as keys to figurative as well as literal meanings of words.[20] In fact, an etymology might be completely metaphoric. To explain the origin of a word was to expose its secret affiliation with things that might normally seem unrelated to it. The Golden Legend, surely one of Chaucer's models for his own Legend, contains hundreds of these metaphorical derivations. In a well-known instance that Chaucer himself versified in the prologue to the Second Nun's Tale, we find: "Cecilia comes from coeli lilia, lily of Heaven, or from caecis via, a way unto the blind. . . ."[21] In the passage from the Prologue quoted above, Chaucer shows how "by reson" the daisy has acquired its name as a result of its physical likeness to the sun. In this case, metaphor and etymology are one.

With both physical and linguistic ties to the sun, Chaucer's daisy emerges as a strikingly appropriate model for the poet's craft. Using this flower's close relationship to "truth," Chaucer dramatically illustrates the nature and function of poetic expression. First, though it is dependent on the sun for nourishment, the daisy still retains a certain humble earthly autonomy, just as good poetry depends on truth to justify its existence, yet has a life of its own, governed by its own rules and appreciated for its own beauty. Second, in form and color the daisy imitates the sun, just as poetry, in both classical and medieval definitions, imitates truth. And third, the word "daisy" is an explicit metaphor, demonstrating an alternative, oblique way of conveying the meaning "sun" in much the same way that Chaucer had previously expressed it in the Troilus—"the dayes honour, and the hevenes yë,/ The nyghtes foo—al this clepe I the sonne" (2.904–5). Thus the mediating function of poetry is

[20]Judson Boyce Allen in The Friar as Critic (Nashville: Vanderbilt Univ. Press, 1971) says, "The fundamental key to the meaning of words, and therefore of verbal integumenta is etymology. . . . This is of course true . . . for the entire middle ages" (p. 15). John of Salisbury defines etymology as a "resemblance of words" and "analysis; analogy of words" (Metalogicon, trans. Daniel D. McGarry [1955; rpt. Gloucester: Peter Smith, 1971], p. 255).

[21]Jacobus de Voragine, The Golden Legend, trans. Granger Ryan and Helmut Ripperger (1941; rpt. New York: Arno Press, 1969), p. 689.

made vivid and explicit in the figure of Chaucer's flower, whose powers of representation are truly extraordinary.[22]

Finally, because the daisy explicitly performs this mediating function in Chaucer's Prologue, we can explain why the narrator venerates it with language drawn from devotional verse addressed to the Virgin Mary. The daisy's gentle light, its worthiness as an earthly object of adoration and love, and its power to mediate between earth and heaven are all attributes of Mary that link her with the daisy and later with Alceste. It is important to realize that Chaucer is asking his readers to notice this parallel: his daisy performs the same intercessory role in the poetic model that Mary performs in the theological one. She intercedes on behalf of humans in the face of God; the daisy intercedes on behalf of viewers in the face of the sun. Even more specifically, both Mary and the daisy have connections with sunlight; like the daisy, Mary was seen as a gentle conveyor of sunlight to earth, for she hid within her the bright sun that was Christ.[23] The daisy's identity as a metaphor has further relevance to the mariological tradition. More than any other Christian figure, Mary attracted metaphorical epithets, such as *stella*

---

[22]For an interesting modern viewpoint on metaphor and sun following, see Jacques Derrida's "White Mythology," trans. F. C. T. Moore, *New Literary History*, 6 (Autumn, 1974), 5–74, which discusses the heliotrope as the perfect "metaphor of the metaphor" (pp. 46–60). The essay also discusses the sun as a metaphor for inexpressible truth.

[23]See Yrjö Hirn, *The Sacred Shrine* (Boston: Beacon Press, 1957), pp. 466–67: "When the Saviour had once been looked upon as a sun, His mother naturally had her counterpart in that which enclosed the sun. The sun is often hidden in clouds; therefore Mary is the cloud which hides the great light. . . . Thus to theologians and poets Mary became the 'light cloud,' which bore the Saviour in its womb. . . . Her being shines with divine light in the same way that the clouds are shone through by the sun. . . ." Hirn mentions several medieval writers who used this analogy, among them Bernard of Clairvaux, *Sermo I, De adventu Domini, PL* 183, col. 39, and Gualterus Wiburnus in his *Encomium Beatae Mariae*, in *Analecta Hymnica Medii Aevi* 1, ed. Clemens Blume and Guido Maria Dreves (Leipzig, 1886), p. 631. Also, Albertus Magnus calls Mary a "cloud which tempers and obscures the sun in order to accommodate man's vision. She does this in a three-fold way: by giving Christ flesh, by tempering justice with mercy, and by being an object of meditation less dazzling than Christ" (*De laudibus Beatae Mariae Virginis*, quoted in Dunbar, p. 276). Also note the description of Mary as the fair garden that flowers under the rays of Christ, *Paradiso* 23.70–73, and as the moon, which "receives and makes something of the light of the divine sun, whether in mediation" or in the "realization and fulfillment of its own blessedness" (Patricia M. Kean, *The Pearl: An Interpretation* [New York: Barnes and Noble, 1967], p. 147).

maris, hortus conclusus, and *regina coeli.*[24] Geoffrey of Vinsauf, a twelfth-century rhetorician, even applies one of her traditional epithets, the "clear cloud," to poetry, explaining that certain figures of speech obliquely transmit "light."[25] Both Mary and metaphor, then, are links between earth and heaven. Both intercede on behalf of fallen humanity—Mary in the theological hierarchy, the daisy (and later its personification Alceste) in the secular, poetic one.

As comic as Chaucer's Prologue may be, we must not overlook the serious point that he is making: that intercessors are as necessary in matters of human perception as they are in matters of salvation. Written sources of truth play a crucial role in the human quest for knowledge. We cannot all be experienced lovers—or for that matter travelers or philosophers or theologians gifted with mystical visitations. Consequently we must depend on literature and its symbolism to make accessible to us the wisdom our limited experience cannot promise to give. Written perhaps in response to the onset of a new age of experience, an age in which scientists were rapidly becoming experimenters and philosophers were defending direct experiential evidence as a beginning for our understanding of the world

[24]For an exhaustive list of Mary's metaphorical epithets, see J. P. Migne, *PL* 219, Index Marianus, cols. 495–528.

[25]About one of the tropes that require oblique rather than direct expression, Geoffrey writes: "This manner of skillful expression can enclose the whole strength of a discourse in half a statement. A statement thus born does not arrive at beautiful colors openly but reveals itself through signs. It shines indirectly, nor does it wish to proceed directly into the light" (*The Poetria Nova and Its Sources in Early Rhetorical Doctrine,* ed. and trans. Ernest Gallo [The Hague: Mouton, 1971], ll. 1583–87. Here Geoffrey implies that this figure both generates its own indirect light and simultaneously indicates a light greater than itself, toward which it proceeds in the same indirect way. In another passage, Geoffrey uses the same analogy to discuss a list of other tropes, writing, "A certain decoration of style and a certain kind of gravity are present in the above forms, which arise when the subject does not appear publicly with its face unveiled, nor does its own but rather an alien expression serve it; and thus, as it were, it covers itself with a cloud—but a clear cloud" (Gallo, ll. 1051–55). See also Margaret F. Nims, "*Translatio:* 'Difficult Statement' in Medieval Poetic Theory," *University of Toronto Quarterly,* 43 (Spring, 1974), 219: "A metaphor is, we might say, a minimal *involucrum;* it is unlike the usual *involucrum,* however, in that its wrapping is diaphanous." Also, the "clear cloud" closely resembles Spenser's metaphor for allegory, "shadowes light." See the Prologue to Book 2 of *The Faerie Queene,* stanza 5.

around us, the *Legend*'s Prologue wisely argues that many a thing is true "thogh every wight ne may it nat ysee" (F, G 15). The *Legend* is a tribute to the poets who have kept those "true things" alive in the works they have written for the inexperienced to read. Chaucer addresses them gratefully in his poem because he sees them as essential links in the important cultural process of passing on truths to future generations. His own case illustrates the point:

> And thogh it happen me rehercen eft
> That ye han in your fresshe songes sayd,
> Forbereth me, and beth nat evele apayd,
> Syn that ye see I do yt in the honour
> Of love, and eke in service of the flour
> Whom that I serve as I have wit or myght.
> [F 78–83, G 66–70]

Chaucer's appropriation of material from others' "fresshe songes" is not selfish theft, but an attempt first to honor love and then to serve the flower that "figures," that is, to respect the subject matter that deserves permanence in the poetic tradition and then to glorify the model in which all art finds its best ultimate defense. Regardless of their particular affiliations with the flower and leaf debate, the frivolous controversy that engaged *marguerite* poets throughout the fourteenth century, all poets are asked to see how they will benefit from Chaucer's praise and understanding of his little daisy:

> But helpeth, ye that han konnyng and myght,
> Ye lovers that kan make of sentement;
> In this cas oghte ye be diligent
> To forthren me somwhat in my labour,
> Whethir ye ben with the leef or with the flour.
> [F 68–72]

Written in honor of love and in service of the daisy, Chaucer's *Legend* rewards all poets with the acclaim they deserve.

— 2 —

Metaphor, Alceste, and the God of Love

As we observed in the last chapter, Alceste's identity as poetry is based on many of the attributes visible in the daisy our narrator worships in the predream sequence of events. The flower's shape, color, light, and heliotropism all contribute to its essential function as an imitator of the sun, an earthly version, if you will, of some heavenly truth. But the connection between the daisy and poetry is best conveyed by the metaphorical name of the flower. The name "daisy," or "day's eye," actually functions in a way similar to poetry—that is, it names clearly yet indirectly the thing it symbolizes. To the modern reader, accustomed to viewing the figures of speech as verbal tricks capable of producing different—though equally powerful—effects, the fact that Chaucer characterizes his flower as a metaphor (and not some other device) may seem immaterial. In the medieval period, however, this particular figure of speech had far greater importance to poetic theory than it has today. Indeed, it would be safe to say that the medieval theory of poetry was to a large extent dependent upon the understanding of how metaphors work, and Chaucer's *Legend* is indebted to the rich rhetorical tradition that named metaphor—to borrow a phrase from Chaucer himself—as the "emperice and flour of floures alle" (F 185).

Metaphor did not always hold the important place it came to occupy in medieval rhetorical thought. Its growth from a simple trope in the classical rhetorical treatises to a symbol of the poetic method in medieval ones was gradual. In fact, until the time of Quintilian's *Institutio oratoria*, metaphor (*translatio* in Latin) did not receive any special treatment or analysis in Roman treatises on rhetoric and the figures of speech. In the *Rhetorica ad Herennium*, for example, one of the most influential works on the art from the Ciceronian tradition, the author includes metaphor near the end of a long list of tropes such as hyperbole, onomatopoeia, and periphrasis, noting only that these figures are special because they demonstrate how language "departs from the ordinary meaning of the words and is with a certain grace applied in another sense."[1] Even when it comes time to define *translatio*, the author of the *Rhetorica* appears to understate its usefulness when he says that its transfer in meaning occurs "because the similarity seems to justify this transference."[2] In concluding his discussion of *translatio*, he names six occasions when a writer might need it: for vividness, brevity, embellishment, magnification, diminution, and to avoid obscenity.[3]

Quintilian, on the other hand, in his *Institutio oratoria* (ca. A.D. 92), chooses to begin his list of tropes with metaphor, saying that it far surpasses the others in beauty:

> Let us begin, then, with the commonest and by far the most beautiful of tropes, namely the metaphor, the Greek term for our *translatio*. . . . It is in itself so attractive and elegant that however distinguished the language in which it is embedded it shines forth with a light that is all its own.[4]

---

[1]*Rhetorica ad Herennium*, trans. Harry Caplan (Cambridge, Mass.: Harvard Univ. Press, 1968), 4.31.42. On the classical distinction between figures and tropes, see Quintilian, *Institutio oratoria*, trans. H. E. Butler, 4 vols. (New York: G. P. Putnam's, Loeb Classical Library, 1921), 8.2.44–47. The former referred to a play on a group of words, a whole sentence, or a paragraph; the latter referred to a play on a single word only.
[2]4.39.45.
[3]4.34.45.
[4]8.6.4.

He continues by saying that tropes such as these "help out our meaning" and "concern not merely individual words but also our thoughts and the structure of our sentences."[5] Before he finishes his description of *translatio*, he divides it into four major types and includes examples to help the reader recognize its wide application. The four types are a transference (1) of the characteristics of one inanimate object to another, (2) of inanimate characteristics to living creatures, (3) of the characteristics of one living creature to another, and (4) of animate characteristics to an inanimate object.[6] About the last, Quintilian writes:

> But above all, effects of extraordinary sublimity are produced when the theme is exalted by a bold and almost hazardous metaphor and inanimate objects are given life and action.[7]

In short, Quintilian's respect for metaphor's versatility and power resulted in the first extended analysis of what happens when writers employ the "meaning transfer" of metaphorical language, especially that which creates "new life" through personification.

Quintilian's influence was felt by later rhetoricians and grammarians including Donatus, whose *Ars grammatica* became the standard medieval textbook on grammar and usage. Although he lists more tropes than Quintilian does, Donatus classifies them in the same way. Metaphor, with its four permutations of the animate/inanimate categories, comes first.[8] But Donatus also defines metaphor as a transference of words and things —a definition that found its way into several later medieval treatises on tropes, including that of Bede, who writes, *Metaphora est rerum verborumque translatio*.[9] Metaphor thus began

[5]8.6.2.
[6]8.6.9–12.
[7]8.6.11.
[8]*Ars Grammatica*, in *Grammatici Latini*, ed. H. Keil, 7 vols. (Leipzig, 1855–70), 3:399.
[9]*Ars Grammatica*, 3:399. For Bede, see *De Schematibus et Tropis*, PL 90, cols. 175–86. Metaphor is in col. 179. There is a translation by Gussie Hecht Tannenhaus, *Quarterly Journal of Speech*, 48 (October, 1962), 237–53.

to receive attention as an important and versatile artistic tool.[10] Even in short manuals and lists of tropes like Bede's, the effect of metaphor on readers was described as part of the cognitive process of moving from words to the things they signify and from things to the divine realities they in turn represent. By the mid–twelfth century, John of Salisbury even stated that words and things exchanged qualities by means of figurative speech:

This reciprocity between things and words, and words and things, whereby they mutually communicate their qualities, as by an exchange of gifts, is more commonly accomplished by words used in a metaphorical sense [translativis sermonibus] than by those of secondary origin. . . . This force of transferred meaning, whereby properties of things are ascribed to words, and vice versa, gives birth to a certain tolerance, which permits the use of words in varying senses.[11]

Such recognition of the unusual powers of metaphorical language gave translatio high priority in the twelfth-century treatises on rhetoric known as the artes poetriae. For example, in the Ars versificatoria, Matthew of Vendôme writes:

This trope, by a kind of special prerogative, enjoys a unique preeminence over all tropes and ought to be used by verse writers especially, for it confers a peculiar charm upon metrical composition.[12]

And in the Documentum de modo et arte dictandi et versificandi, a prose rendering of the Poetria nova, Geoffrey of Vinsauf includes a long and detailed section on the "art of making metaphors." Here Geoffrey adds his own ideas about translatio, first by reducing Quintilian's four categories to two: the transfer-

[10]It was, of course, still discussed as a trope useful for decoration alone.
[11]Metalogicon, trans. McGarry, p. 50. For what John means by "secondary origin" see McGarry's note, p. 50.
[12]Edmond Faral, ed., Les arts poétiques de XIIe et du XIIIe siècles (Paris: Lib. Honoré Champion, 1958), p. 173.

ence of nonhuman qualities to humans, and of human qualities to nonhuman things.[13] Like Quintilian, Geoffrey prefers the latter type of *translatio*, transferring human qualities to things, because it is easier to understand and create. In advising beginning writers on the construction of this kind of *translatio*, Geoffrey clearly shows that it is a form of personification, closely related to the construction of allegorical characters.[14] This kind of *translatio*, of human qualities to things, is, of course, the kind that governs the *Legend*'s Prologue; during the transformation that takes place between the narrator's waking and sleeping, the daisy is given human life as Alceste.

Figurative language, of which metaphor is the most important example, was categorized in the late medieval period as an essential component of allegorical expression. Figures of speech were considered the primary constituents of poetry, because on the level of the individual figure there occurred the workings of poetry in miniature, the indirect disclosure of meaning. Defenders of the art of poetry often compared it to Scripture, noting that poetry and Scripture contained the same kinds of indirect and figurative expression.[15] Petrarch even goes so far as to equate poetry with theology on the basis of

[13]*Documentum de modo et arte dictandi et versificandi*, trans. Roger P. Parr, Mediaeval Philosophical Texts in Translation, no. 17 (Milwaukee: Marquette Univ. Press, 1968), pp. 61–62.

[14]*Documentum*, p. 62. Also see Gallo's remarks in *Poetria nova*, pp. 204–5. The *Rhetorica ad Herennium* defines allegory in the same way (4.34.46), though "allegory" itself had not yet gained the important status it held in medieval thought. Marcia Colish in *The Mirror of Language*, p. 17, writes that the *aenigma* of 1 Corinthians 13 was considered a species of metaphor. Margaret Nims, in "*Translatio*," p. 229n., writes, "Cicero and Quintilian and their medieval followers defined the trope *allegoria* as an expanded metaphor or metaphor-series. In relation to this allegory of the rhetoricians, and later the allegory of the poets, metaphor is a basic allegoreme." Also see Rosamund Tuve, *Elizabethan and Metaphysical Imagery* (Chicago: Univ. of Chicago Press, 1947), p. 105: "*Allegoria* does not use metaphor; it is one."

[15]In an article on Petrarch's poetics, Concetta Carestia Greenfield writes, "Petrarch defends the obscurity of poetical allegory, likening it to that of Scriptural allegory. Following the Augustinian argument, he says that the divine word must be obscure, for it is the expression of an inconceivable power, access to which must be rendered difficult to make its understanding pleasing and wondrous" ("The Poetics of Francis Petrarch," in *Francis Petrarch, Six Centuries Later*, North Carolina Studies in the Romance Languages and Literatures 3 [Chapel Hill: Univ. of North Carolina Press, 1975], p. 219).

their sharing figurative speech, "whose main element is the metaphor."[16] Margaret Nims, noting the medieval preoccupation with metaphor, rightly concludes that this trope best characterizes poetry's methods in general. Quoting Vincent of Beauvais, she writes:

> The office of the poet, specifically, is "to transpose the events of life into new shapes, employing with skill and charm oblique figurative modes." It would seem that the *translatio* that is metaphor underlies the *transformatio*, the *transfiguratio*, that is poetry. As a small but complete act of *obliqua figuratio*, metaphor appears to be a basic unit of verbal making—of *poesis*, of *mimesis*. Metaphor, we might say, is a poeseme.[17]

In the *artes poetriae*, metaphor appears to have transcended its origins as merely one of many tropes and to have come to represent the way poets communicate abstract meaning in concrete terms.

The recognition that *translatio* has a significant and well-defined role in poetic theory prompted many medieval writers to caution poets against using verbal ornamentation as mere outward show. A good metaphor, writes Geoffrey of Vinsauf, will fulfill its potential to convey meaning; in his words, it will have a mind as well as a face.[18] Figures must not be used indiscriminately or for decoration only, but must serve a purpose by contributing to a poem's *sententia*. In the *Poetria nova*, Geoffrey states:

> Unless the inner ornament conforms to the outer requirement, the relationship between the two is worthless. Painting only the face of an expression results in a vile picture, a falsified thing, a faked form, a whitewashed wall, a verbal hypocrite which pretends to be something when it is nothing. Its form covers up its deformity; it vaunts itself outwardly but has no inner substance.[19]

[16]Greenfield, p. 218.
[17]Nims, p. 221.
[18]*Poetria nova* 744–45.
[19]*Poetria nova* 742–53.

Here, and in passages from the *Documentum*, Geoffrey's remarks amount to a definition of what a good metaphor is. Specifically, it aids the reader in moving from the verbal surface of a poem to the meaning intended by its writer. It exists not for its own sake, but rather to effect that special exchange between words and things. Good metaphors demonstrate intrinsic and objective (though perhaps hidden) similarities between things; they are not arbitrary creations meant only to adorn a poet's work. Dante in the *Vita Nuova* agrees: "For it would be a disgrace to someone who dressed his rhymes in the figures or colors of rhetoric if later, on demand, he could not strip his discourse of this dress to show what he had really meant."[20]

In light of these remarks, it seems clear that Chaucer selected this particular flower, the daisy, because it demonstrates how successful metaphors work, following guidelines very similar to those suggested by Geoffrey of Vinsauf and Dante. In other words, Chaucer's daisy survives scrutiny even when its ability to carry meaning is subjected to rigorous testing. In conveying the meaning "sun," the daisy first communicates the verbal likeness between the two objects being compared; the fact that the daisy and the sun share a name might constitute the decorative surface of the metaphor, the part that Geoffrey calls its "face." But even without this linguistic "dress," there is a second reason for the validity of the metaphor, and that is the physical resemblance of the daisy and the sun. Thus the daisy "means" the sun, both *in verbo* and *in re*.

Alceste, the personification of the daisy in Chaucer's dream, carries on the daisy's physical resemblance to the sun. The ladies who attend her, venerating her for her truth in love, openly recognize her full validity as a flower that "figures":

> "Heel and honour
> To trouthe of womanhede, and to this flour
> That bereth our alder pris in figurynge!
> Hire white corowne bereth the witnessynge."
> [F 296–99]

---

[20]Chap. 25, in *The Literary Criticism of Dante Alighieri*, trans. Robert S. Haller, pp. 117–18.

Alceste's white crown bears witness to her likeness to the daisy, with its white circle around the center of the flower. And it is this crown, or white circle, that also bears witness to Alceste's natural imitation of the sun.[21] As the visual basis that lends validity to *translatio*, Alceste's crown demonstrates that effective metaphorical language finds its basis in reality, not in a fabricated or falsified likeness. Furthermore, if we wish to carry the metaphor further, we may interpret Alceste's crown in one of its classical senses, as the prize given to one who has performed outstanding poetic achievements.[22] After all, the ladies are praising Alceste for bearing the "alder pris in figurynge."

Another quality of metaphor which relates to the characterization of Alceste in the *Legend*'s Prologue is the fact that it (and finally poetry, which metaphor here symbolizes) is a vehicle, a means to an end. As a reader processes a metaphorical expression, his mind moves from the figure itself to the "higher truth" the figure was created to convey. Describing this process, Margaret Nims writes (accidentally employing apt Chaucerian terms) that a metaphor "opens, flowers, and dies; its life and luminosity are transferred to the term for whose sake it was made."[23] There is thus something sacrificial about metaphors, functioning as they do primarily as vehicles for things greater than themselves. Their lives, though short, are full of significance, but once they have performed the duty of semantic transfer, they are no longer useful to readers, and they "die." No long leap need be taken for us to see in this paradigm the outline of Alcestis's life as it appears in classical accounts and in Chaucer's own brief sketch of her biography. Alcestis willingly died to permit her husband a longer life, thus sacrificing herself for what she, at least, considered a "greater good." She remained in the Underworld until Hercules recognized her vir-

---

[21] See *Thesaurus Linguae Latinae* (Leipzig: Teubner, 1806–9), which defines *corona* in its primary sense as *margaritum -ae* (i.e., "daisy"). Alceste's crown has other meanings as well which are central to her complex identity. It is the *corona* of the sun (*TLL* 3.B.2.a) and the crown of martyrdom (Lewis and Short, *A Latin Dictionary*, s.v. *corona*, 1.2)

[22] *TLL*, s.v. *corona*, 2.A, "de laude poetica."

[23] Nims, p. 219.

tue and was able, as part of one of his labors, to bring her back
to life. The story is told quickly in the *Legend*'s Prologue:

> "Hastow nat in a book, lyth in thy cheste,
> The grete goodnesse of the quene Alceste . . .
> She that for hire housbonde chees to dye,
> And eke to goon to helle, rather than he,
> And Ercules rescowed hire, parde,
> And broght hir out of helle agayn to blys?"
>
> [F 510–16]

Like the Alcestis of myth, Chaucer's "dayesye" dies in the selfless act of giving life to something else—the very process that
metaphor, indeed all literature, undergoes. And to underscore
the close correlation between Alceste and the flower, Chaucer
has the narrator link them in the lines that immediately follow
the rehearsal of the Alcestis legend. In answer to the God of
Love's question (F 510–16), the narrator replies,

> "Now knowe I hire. And is this good Alceste,
> The dayesie, and myn owene hertes reste?
> Now fele I weel the goodnesse of this wyf,
> That both aftir hir deth and in hir lyf
> Hir grete bounte doubleth hire renoun.
> Wel hath she quyt me myn affeccioun,
> That I have to hire flour, the dayesye."
>
> [F 517–24]

Finally, Chaucer alters the end of the Alcestis story to make
even clearer the analogy between her life and the process by
which literature discloses meaning. Mentioning again the daisy's "white corowne," the narrator tells of Alceste's final and
most impressive "translation" into a star:

> "No wonder ys thogh Jove hire stellyfye,
> As telleth Agaton, for hire goodnesse!
> Hire white corowne berith of hyt witnesse. . . ."[24]
>
> [F 525–27]

[24]On "Agaton," see Robinson, *Works*, p. 846n.

This alternative destiny, in which Chaucer has Jove reward Alcestis for her selfless deed by giving her a permanent place in the heavens is a fitting reward for this metaphorical lady, because Chaucer is allowing her to take on the actual identity of some heavenly truth her transitory life was given up for. Though she cannot become the sun (there is only one, of course, and it stands for God), she is given the second best identity that heaven has to offer—that of a bright eternal star, a diminutive sun, if you will, but one that will shine forever.

As we have seen so far, all the characters and concepts with which Chaucer is working are derived from the natural world. The daisy, the sun, and Alceste's star all are drawn from his observation of nature's orderly patterns: the bright sun rises and sets, the daisy imitates that action because it is wholly dependent on light, and the star resembles a mini-sun that shines with enough gentle illumination to make this "derke world" (F 85) a little less gloomy. In his insistence upon nature as the source of his art Chaucer is strongly acknowledging the medieval idea that the foundations of "symbolic truths" were to be discovered in reality. According to the medieval theorists of art who were connected with the school of Chartres, natural objects "signified" divine realities in much the same way that texts (the Bible in particular) signified things other than their literal levels might suggest.[25] An object's literal existence contained something like divine transcendence, and to perceive an object's full significance was a matter of moving from its earthly qualities to its transcendent ones. These twelfth-century writers found the rhetorical process of *translatio* to be an ideal descriptive model. The way in which the Chartrians understood the world was closely analogous to the way in which they read and interpreted the *figurae* in a text. M.-D. Chenu, the modern expert on this medieval idea, sums it up as follows: "*Translatio* [is] a transference or elevation from the visible sphere to the in-

---

[25]Most medievalists agree that there was a distinct group of theorists who shared an interest in synthesizing rhetoric and theology and that they were all connected in some way to the school of Chartres. But see R. W. Southern, "Humanism and the School of Chartres," in *Medieval Humanism and Other Studies* (Oxford: Blackwell, 1970), pp. 61–85.

visible through the mediating agency of an image borrowed from sense perceptible reality. This is what we mean by 'metaphor.'"[26]

The respect for *literalness*, both in texts and in life, shared by all Chartrian thinkers is particularly important to Chaucer's beliefs about art. The material basis from which *translatio* proceeds is essential to its operation and must never be viewed as either superfluous or inferior as a level of divine expression. Père Chenu expresses this idea well:

> The symbol, in order to effect the transference for which it is the vehicle, calls for matter which does not disappear in the process of signifying, such, for example, as the reality of the natural elements. . . . [Symbolic] values emerge only in proportion as the *res* retains its integrity while functioning as *signum*. In turning reality into nothing but a figure, tropology weakens itself. Such an insistence underlay the great undertakings of Hugh of St. Victor, who asserted the prior necessity of the *fundamentum* before *allegoria*, of the truth of *historia* before *tropi*. Moralization . . . ended up in attenuated abstraction, for it dissolved the natural or historical materials upon which it operated, even as in former days it dissolved the myths of the pagans.[27]

Yet there was a distinct tendency for medieval readers and writers to allegorize without respect for literal meaning, a tendency that attracted comment from the Chartrians.[28] Several times in the *Metalogicon*, John of Salisbury, for example, expresses disdain for those who do not respect the "literalness" of what they read: "What he now teaches, Cornificius learned at a time when there was no 'letter' in liberal studies, and everyone sought the 'spirit,' which, so they tell us, lies hidden in the letter";[29] and "a trustworthy and prudent reader will respect as

---

[26]M.-D. Chenu, "The Symbolist Mentality," in *Nature, Man, and Society in the Twelfth Century: Essays on New Theological Perspectives in the Latin West*, trans. Jerome Taylor and Lester K. Little (Chicago: Univ. of Chicago Press, 1968), p. 138.

[27]Chenu, pp. 132–33.

[28]Chenu, pp. 141–42.

[29]*Metalogicon*, p. 14.

inviolable the evident literal meaning of what is written, until he obtains a fuller and surer grasp of the truth."[30] Chaucer's miniature enactment in the *Legend*'s Prologue of the process by which the earthly daisy "means" the heavenly sun is, I think, a strong defense, by analogy, of the inviolability of textual literalness.[31] Chaucer honors the daisy's humble earthly autonomy because by doing so he is able to express his enduring commitment to the value of "realistic" poetry, poetry that treats common earthly creatures as worthy of the artist's closest attention. This idea, as it is expressed in the *Legend*'s Prologue thus helps us identify the origins of one of Chaucer's most notable traits, his characteristic interest in reflecting what is true to life.

Throughout these first two chapters, I have attempted to show Chaucer's belief that figures of speech, and a poet's fictions in general, if they reflect something real, are highly serviceable (and easily defended) vehicles of Christian truth. I have praised Alceste—the embodiment of Chaucer's art—for her ability to synthesize earth and heaven (she is both daisy and sun at once) and have seen in her a powerful vindication of the complex process by which poets convey real truths. In short, for the purposes of clarifying the *Legend*'s main issues, I have made some generalizations about Chaucer's thought that now need appropriate qualification. Though Chaucer is defending in his *Legend* the validity of poetic figures, he is far from calling for a *dolce stil nuovo* that uses unrestrained figuration or a multitude of rarefied personifications such as one might find in the cosmological poems of the Chartrian school. He was surely aware that figures of speech (metaphor included) are capable of seriously distorting the issues they are meant to serve; that they, more than any other rhetorical device, involve the circumlocution of truth. As Donatus, Servius, Priscian, Isidore, Cassiodorus, and Bede realized before him, because figures of

---

[30]*Metalogicon*, p. 148.

[31]Anthony Nemetz, in "Literalness and the *Sensus Litteralis*," *Speculum*, 34 (1959), p. 76, notes that medieval writers categorized figures of speech as part of the literal levels of texts. Judson Allen in *The Friar as Critic*, p. 84, agrees, adding that etymologies too are part of the literal level.

speech are circumlocutions, even good ones can severely obfuscate truth if they are not fully understood by their readers.[32]
We need not accuse Chaucer's daisy-Alceste of promoting such
obfuscation, however; the poet labored hard to construct his
figure so that it would have unambiguous significance. But we
do need to take a closer look at the God of Love.

Although the God of Love's sunlike visage helped us locate
Chaucer's Prologue within an important poetic and epistemological tradition, we have not yet begun to ask how he himself
fits into the scheme his shining face invokes. It is easiest to begin the investigation of this deity's identity by ruling out what
he definitely is *not*. First, the God of Love is not the sun, even
though he carries its emblem on his crown. Chaucer is careful
to point out that the real sun is an entity existing separate and
apart from this deity. Late in the F Prologue the God of Love
notices the sun setting, an indication to him that it is time to go
home:

> "I mot goon hom (the sonne draweth west)
> To paradys, with al this companye. . . ."
>
> [563–64]

Furthermore, with regard to the God of Love's own light, it is
clear that he is crowned with *a* sun, not *the* sun. And in the
lines that describe his bright face, we discover on close reading

[32]These classical and medieval writers are listed in the *Metalogicon*, p. 57, as
spokesmen for the obscurity of figurative language. To this list one should add
Aristotle, who advises disputants to pay close attention to their opponents'
words in argumentation: "See if he has used a metaphorical expression . . . for
a metaphorical expression is always obscure," *Topics*, trans. W. A. Pickard-Cam-
bridge, *The Works of Aristotle*, 12 vols. (Oxford: Oxford Univ. Press, 1908–52),
6.2.139B. Augustine also realized the difficulties raised by figurative language;
his *De doctrina Christiana* had as its object the outlining of strategies by which
readers could clarify ambiguous figurative expression. John of Salisbury, too,
writes that figurative speech "confounds and virtually slays the uneducated,
preventing them from comprehending the truth" (*Metalogicon*, p. 50), and
"The combining process of the intellect, whereby things that are not united are
copulated, lacks objectivity, but its abstracting process is both accurate and true
to reality. [This] constitutes, as it were, the common factory of art" (*Metalogicon*,
p. 120). John also names rhetorical tropes as an aspect of language which inter-
feres with easy access to meaning (*Metalogicon*, p. 56). Obviously, medieval distrust of figurative language runs deep.

that when compared to the light of the real sun, his is negligible indeed:

> His gilte heer was corowned with a sonne,
> Instede of gold, for hevynesse and wyghte.
> Therwith me thoghte his face shoon so bryghte
> That wel unnethes myghte I him beholde. . . .
>
> [F 230–33]

The word "unnethes" implies that beholding this face is hard to do—but not impossible. And in G, Chaucer comically reveals to us his exact calculations concerning the range at which the God of Love's light dazzles:

> For sikerly his face shon so bryghte
> That with the glem astoned was the syghte;
> A furlong-wey I myhte hym not beholde.
>
> [G 163–65]

In other words, the beams from the God of Love's face can impair the vision of a man two hundred yards away, but when compared to the long distance traveled by the brilliant light of the real sun, a "furlong-wey" is hardly a length worth measuring. Obviously, Chaucer is forcing us to discredit any notion that links the God of Love too closely with the sun.

Moreover, the God of Love cannot be very closely identified with the Cupid of the classical world, although he has wings and carries fiery darts. Cupid is always·represented as sightless, but not so this Chaucerian deity; the narrator indicates that this God of Love seems to have vision:

> And al be that men seyn that blynd ys he,
> Algate me thoghte that he myghte se;
> For sternely on me he gan byholde,
> So that his loking dooth myn herte colde.[33]
>
> [F 237–40, G 167–72]

[33]On Cupid's blindness in medieval iconography, see Erwin Panofsky, "Blind Cupid," in *Studies in Iconology* (1939; rpt. New York: Harper and Row, 1972), pp. 95–128.

Finally, although he seems to resemble a flower in some respects, with his daisylike crown, his "green-greved" torso, and
his self-conscious heliotropism as he tells time by the sun, his
outfit is much too artificial to be identified as nature's simple
handiwork. His cloak is wrought from costly silk and orna-
mented with artful embroidery:

> Yclothed was this myghty god of Love
> In silk, enbrouded ful of grene greves,
> In-with a fret of rede rose-leves,
> The fresshest syn the world was first bygonne.
>
> [F 226–29, G 158–61]

It is worth noting that this God of Love's garments are much
fancier than those worn by the deities of love in French works
of fiction and are thus meant to distinguish him from the natural, vegetative gods that may have served originally as Chaucer's models. In the *Romance of the Rose*, for example, the
author states explicitly that the deity's cloak is *not* made out
of silk, but instead out of natural flowers gleaned from the
springtime fields.[34] Chaucer's God of Love, on the other hand,
bears the unmistakable stamp of artificiality—even dandy-
ism—that stands in marked contrast to the natural simplicity
of Chaucer's lady the daisy. For Alceste, who keeps the daisy's
humble cloak even though her poet has bestowed upon her the
honor of human life, is merely "clothed al in grene" (F 242,
341; G 174). Moreover, her outward appearance does not suggest that she has affiliations to any other object than what she,
in reality, actually is. As Chaucer notes about her, "she kytheth
what she ys" (F 504, G 492). In contrast, the God of Love has
borrowed the attributes of sun and daisy both, not to mention
the demeanor and judgmental role of the Christian God,
whose imposing presence he strives to mimic at every turn. On

---

[34]In Chaucer's translation, the lines read, "This God of Love of his fasoun /
Was lyk no knave, ne quystroun; / His beaute greatly was to pryse. / But of his
robe to devise / I drede encombred for to be; / For nought yclad in silk was
he, / But all in floures and flourettes. . ." (ll. 885–91).

top of this confusion, his having the wings and darts of Cupid serves only to obfuscate further the ultimate identity of this eclectic god, who is finally not the sun, Cupid, God, or the daisy he slyly impersonates.

The most telling fact about the God of Love, however, is that he does not—and cannot—exist outside Chaucer's dream. No hint of him whatsoever appears in the narrator's natural surroundings, even though they are described in detail before the dream begins. The God of Love's absence from the real world casts doubt upon his ability to signify truth of any kind, and it finally shows that he is intended to stand as an example of a literary abstraction, one with no roots in reality at all. As a character whose metaphorical attributes do not add up to a clear representation of any real truth, and thus as a character who can survive only in dream visions and not in descriptions of life, the God of Love is a parody of the kind of poetic artifice that Chaucer wished to reject. The world contains no example of what the God of Love is trying to express; there is no such thing as a "Christian Cupid" in the natural world. Unlike Alceste, who is faithfully shaped to the pattern of a single natural creature, the God of Love has no "literal level" to sustain him, no foundation in the truth, and any resemblance between him and the real world is merely factitious. He is a nonce fabrication, a character who mimics the daisy's natural rhythms and the sun's bright light so unconvincingly that we are forced to discredit any actual correspondence between him and the natural world he pretends to occupy. As a confusing and ultimately empty figure, the God of Love has no validity of his own and must finally be judged as superfluous, for he adds nothing new to Alceste's convincing synthesis of earth and heaven. The God of Love's false synthesis of earthly and religious verities (God, the daisy, the sun) are only mockeries of *translatio*'s real accomplishments.

Thus by contrasting Alceste and the God of Love, Chaucer makes the serious point that poetry can convey abstractions without being unnecessarily or carelessly abstract in nature itself. In attempting to make his poetry meaningful, a poet should not mistakenly believe that truth can be conveyed only through artificial constructs that have little or no reference to actual life. Instead, a poet should find within the forms of natural things the models on which to base the figures of his art. He will have no difficulty finding such natural models, for (as Chaucer implies) daisies are extremely common, and every one of them translates a bit of heavenly wisdom into a form both suitable and pleasing to earthly eyes. If a poet is careful enough to observe the world around him, he can discover true significance in even the humblest of earthly things.

By making clear his distaste for superfluous poetic abstraction through his characterization of the God of Love, Chaucer also seems to be distancing himself from the medieval "court of love" poems, in which allegorical abstractions—love deities included—people the springtime landscapes of dreaming poet figures. Though the love deities who appear in poems written before Chaucer's *Legend* are not quite as overdrawn as this deity (they aren't as "Christian," they aren't as fancily and artificially dressed, and they aren't as interested in classical poetry), there are enough similarities between them and Chaucer's God of Love that we may surmise that they are probably the models for his subversive parody.[35]

In addition to the portrayal of Alceste and the God of Love, there are other evidences in the *Legend*'s Prologue of Chaucer's sentiments about poetry. For example, the singing birds in Chaucer's Prologue seem to have an uncanny understanding of precisely the kind of hypocrisy that the God of Love exemplifies. Having been betrayed by the fowler, the birds, with new-found wisdom, sing derogatorily about his "sophistrye":

[35]For a thorough summary and analysis of medieval literary "courts of Love," see Neilson, *The Origins and Sources of the Court of Love.* For the deities in the *marguerite* poems, see, for example, Froissart's *Dittié de la flour de la Margherite,* ll. 209–15, and Machaut's *Dit de la Margherite,* ll. 123–29. See also Froissart's *Paradys d'Amour,* ll. 970–1500, a possible source for some aspects of Chaucer's plot in the *Legend*'s Prologue, as Lowes suggests in "The Prologue to the *LGW* as Related to the French Marguerite Poems," pp. 642–58. Finally, see H. C. Goddard, who argues that the Prologue is designed to parody its French sources, "Chaucer's *Legend of Good Women,* II," *JEGP,* 8 (1909), 106.

In his dispit hem thoghte yt did hem good
To synge of hym, and in hir song despise
The foule cherl that, for his coveytise,
Had hem betrayed with his sophistrye.
This was hire song, "The foweler we deffye,
And al his craft."

[F 134–39, G 122–26]

Poets who captivate readers by the gleam of worthless verbal ornamentation are guilty of the same kind of "coveytise" as the sophistic hunters. Using what Geoffrey of Vinsauf called "verbal hypocrites" and "faked forms,"[36] they lead readers into a linguistic hall of mirrors where words do nothing but reflect themselves instead of serving, as they ought to, as the vehicle for truth. Once caught in such a labyrinthine trap (one thinks at once of the God of Love's paradoxical identity as God and Cupid both), readers have no hope of escape.[37]

Through the God of Love, Chaucer is also making a statement about easy poetic "solutions" to the difficult problem of reconciling earthly and heavenly love—in particular, the erotic inclinations of classical lovers and the uplifting *caritas* of Christian belief. To be sure, Chaucer himself saw the need for such a synthesis; in the *Troilus* and the *Knight's Tale* he experiments with various ways in which to confirm the religious potential of pagan erotic love. But Chaucer always manages to show this potential without distorting either Christian or pagan beliefs.

[36]On the medieval tradition uniting fowlers and sophists, see Walter Map's *De nugis curialium*: "For it usually happens that birds which do not see the subtle snares or nets believe that there is free passage everywhere. Do not those persons who are occupied all their days with sophistries—men who can ensnare and yet scarce be ensnared and who are ever delvers in the deep abyss—do not these men, in fear of disfavor, profess with reverence to bring forth all things from God, whose dignity is so lofty that no praises or no merits of preachments can attain to that height, unless sovereign mercy has borne them aloft?" This translation is by Frederick Tupper and Marbury Bladen Ogle (London: Chatto and Windus, 1924), p. 76. Also see the fowlers in the *Romance of the Rose*, ll. 21470–513.

[37]See James J. Murphy, *Rhetoric in the Middle Ages* (Berkeley: Univ. of California Press, 1974), p. 60: "The sin of the sophist is that he denies the necessity of subject matter and believes that *forma* alone is desirable."

The narrator of the *Troilus*, for example, is able to use religious language in describing Troilus's devotion to Criseyde without ever forcing Troilus into becoming the Christian he simply was not. And at the end of the *Knight's Tale*, Palamon and Emelye are married in order to fulfill Theseus's remarkable—and almost Christian—hypothesis about a "faire cheyne of love" that binds the First Mover's orderly creation. Yet neither Theseus nor the lovers he unites are ever asked to understand more than they, as pagans, naturally could. Thus though Chaucer clearly wishes to juxtapose and even correlate these two kinds of love, he never assumes them to be derived from the same system of beliefs. His "synthesis," then, is a complicated one, and one that respects the differences between the unrelated values that each culture holds. In the God of Love, however, these two religious systems exist simultaneously. He tries to be Cupid and God at once, in a single, facile union. That is, within the single character of the God of Love we find two incompatible deities, yoked uncomfortably together, who cannot, when judged by any extraliterary standard such as historical or philosophical truth, actually coexist in such a neat, uncomplicated way. Thus the "identity crisis" of Chaucer's God of Love extends beyond the mere fact that he has no "real" origins in the natural world. He has no historical, philosophical, or religious validity either, but stands as an artificial poetic "middleman" created only to make a difficult problem easy.[38]

Dante, too, grappled with this issue when he experimented with his own God of Love, created (like Chaucer's) to unite two "loves" at variance with one another. In the well-known twenty-fifth chapter of the *Vita Nuova*, we learn that the God of Love is a metaphor Dante fashioned to aid the poet in his attempt to understand his relationship to Beatrice and thus ultimately to God. Though the creation of this God of Love was a necessary

[38]Compared to the deities found in other "court of love" poems, Chaucer's God of Love is exaggerated in his Christian attributes. See Neilson, p. 145, and Dodd, pp. 211–12. This exaggeration is, I think, consistent with Chaucer's intention to parody—by overdrawing—the nature of this deity. For a discussion of the "religion of love" poems upon which Chaucer's conception is modeled, see Neilson, pp. 31–34, and 220–27.

step in the young poet's apprenticeship, he finally learns (from the deity himself) that all *simulacra* must be abandoned for a more direct perception of Beatrice and her significant role as mediator between earth and heaven.[39] He discusses the vanity of figures without "substance," that is, without real life, and he deems them unnecessary obfuscations of his true relationship to the actual lady who "figures" better than any abstraction can.[40] I do not mean to suggest that Alceste is Chaucer's Beatrice, for she is clearly less "real" than was Dante's lady. But Chaucer's final rejection of poetic *simulacra* that merely obfuscate, rather than faithfully symbolize, the truth is strikingly similar to Dante's earlier realization about what is very nearly the same issue. Medieval gods of love—including Dante's mighty deity as well as the lesser ones that rule the amatory realms in lighter courtly verse—simply cannot adequately carry out the job they are in theory created to perform, that is, to unite *amor* and *caritas* under a single "law."

A poem that depends for its usefulness entirely on the metaphorical terms surrounding the concept of the "religion of love" was, for Chaucer, a poem that fabricated much too simple a solution to the difficult problems that love poets confronted in their attempts to make narratives about earthly love commensurate with Christian truth. Furthermore, Chaucer did not believe that the creation of a God of Love—an illusory Christian Cupid—was an honest way to appropriate material from

[39]On the vanity of things called "*simulacra*," see Barbara Nolan, "The *Vita Nuova* and Richard of St. Victor's Phenomenology of Vision," *Dante Studies*, 92 (1974), 48–49. On Dante's decision to rid himself of the God of Love, see Robert Hollander, "*Vita Nuova*: Dante's Perceptions of Beatrice," *Dante Studies*, 92 (1974), 6.

[40]Dante's God of Love is a type of metaphor because he is the result of a transference of animate characteristics to something inanimate, the medieval favorite of the four kinds of metaphors. Dante uses exactly those common terms to describe him. One gets the feeling that after Dante had written the famous passage on the importance of having underlying meaning for any metaphor (something as meaningful as creatures with true existences), he realized that his own metaphorical God of Love did not have the significance necessary to vindicate his presence, and thus he quietly abandoned this deity in his later works. See also the lines by Guido Cavalcanti and an anonymous poet about Love's "insubstantiality" which are quoted by Panofsky in "Blind Cupid," *Studies in Iconology*, p. 101.

the classical past, though many poets before him had used this device. By elevating Cupid to a sacred and sovereign lord, poets tried to take an alien classical idea and locate it comfortably within the bounds of traditional medieval thinking. But as Chaucer understood them, such poetic attempts to unite different religions through a single personification could be realized only imperfectly, even though that personification cleverly manifested attributes drawn from both the classical and Christian worlds. There were other, more successful ways to adapt classical amatory texts to poems with courtly, and even thoroughly Christian, concerns. Chaucer's way, as we shall see when we study the *Legend*'s witty dialogue, is embodied in Alceste. For in Alceste, whose identity lies as much with classical antiquity as it does with the poet's common English daisy, we see Chaucer's commitment to using classical fiction, not as it might be tortuously wrenched to fit an alien Christian context, but plainly and simply on its own literary terms. For Chaucer, classical narratives could supply the medieval artist with a variety of stories about love, all of them rich and complicated treatments of a universal human experience under the "law of kynde" that "was and is and ever shall be." And Chaucer's God of Love, who neatly parodies the insubstantial deities of medieval love verse, represents the poet's final farewell to a certain kind of courtly abstraction with which, I suspect, he never felt comfortable.

— 3 —

On Misunderstanding Texts

Even if Chaucer had not chosen to include in his *Legend* the lively and humorous conversation that takes place between the narrator and the two members of the royal amatory court, we would probably still be able to detect the poet's rejection of the simplified courtly characters on which the God of Love is modeled. The deity's physical appearance and his relationship to the daisy and the sun make clear the superfluity and ineffectuality of his role as a figure in poetry. By his presence alone, the God of Love reveals many of the values against which Chaucer was reacting when he wrote the Prologue. But the dialogue that follows the God of Love's arrival adds another dimension to Chaucer's dissatisfaction with the kind of popular poetry that the God of Love represents because it demonstrates the ways in which a reader's approval of such verse actually constitutes an acceptance of erroneous principles of interpretation. The God of Love's specific comments and judgments about Chaucer's poetry reveal him to be an incompetent literary critic, with assumptions so confused that they interfere not only with the correct interpretation of Chaucer's own corpus but, more seriously, with the accurate perception of human experience itself.

As Chaucer was the first to admit, there are many ways to misinterpret a text. Within the *Canterbury Tales* alone, for example, we are asked to entertain a variety of literary responses, both from the pilgrim tellers and from some of the characters within their tales. There are some obvious misreadings, of course, which constitute little more than jokes, such as Chauntecleer's bad translation of Latin in the *Nun's Priest's Tale*. But more important, in the *Tales* there are larger, less easily definable kinds of misinterpretation as well, such as the Wife of Bath's failure to understand the full psychological import of her own tale, or her wildly idiosyncratic readings of some of the written authorities she cites. And Harry Bailly's frequent critical interjections, which are often attempts to conclude the tales he has commissioned with the "sentence" he thinks must be hidden within them, constitute humorous but in some ways understandable misreadings of the narratives he hears. He carelessly moralizes the *Shipman's Tale*, for example, by giving this advice to its listeners: "Draweth no more monkes unto your inn," a comment that adds only a very dubious contribution to our critical understanding of the tale, but that reveals a mind struggling to find within literature the usefulness its defenders always purported it to have.

Unfortunately, besides Harry Bailly, there is no one present on this Canterbury journey to help the pilgrims extract the real wisdom literature has to offer, or to instill within them whatever sound interpretive principles Chaucer may have judged necessary for an informed interpretation of the tales they encounter. With Chaucer's conscious omission of a reliable "reader," either in the person of the narrator or by means of thorough and authoritative glossing by the tellers, the burden of sound interpretation falls on us. Indeed, the objectionably narrow interpretations by some of the pilgrims are specifically designed to exalt our sense that we are superior readers, a sense constantly reinforced by our amusement at detecting (and our self-righteousness at forgiving) the interpretive transgressions of the Canterbury pilgrims.

Not all the voices we hear in the *Canterbury Tales*, however, are those of bad readers. We hear from some discriminating souls as well, both within the tales themselves and among the pilgrim tellers. Dame Prudence in the *Melibee*, for example, tries to teach her husband the virtue of humility, especially in his confrontations with the writings of others. She insistently questions his understanding of written authority with such statements as "I wolde fayn knowe hou ye understonde thilke text, and what is youre sentence" (B 2467). Similarly, the Parson, who has witnessed case after case of reckless interpretation by the time his own turn to speak arrives, chooses to ensure clarity of meaning in his own text by means of frequent paraphrase, patiently introduced with the tag, "that is to seyn." Chaucer's point is not only that people are active and imaginative interpreters of all they read and hear, but also that faulty understanding of a poem's "sentence" is hard to rectify and impossible to prevent. Writers, whether poets or parsons, must be aware of the effects their works may have upon insensitive or, in many cases, merely inexperienced readers, because they themselves are rarely present to arbitrate when their texts meet readers whose critical abilities are wanting. When authors wrote, "Go little book," they knew that they were often bidding farewell to the close kinship between the work and its intended meaning. To his own *Troilus*, of course, Chaucer prays that wherever it is read or sung, it be "understonde" (5.1797–98).

Although Chaucer's interest in how readers construed literary works comes to fruition in the *Canterbury Tales*, where he patiently creates critical viewpoints, he explores this subject first in the *Legend*'s Prologue, where the God of Love offers his unsolicited opinion on some of the poet's works, most of his criticism being directed at *Troilus and Criseyde*. To be sure, the dramatic action making up this section of the *Legend*'s Prologue is a masterpiece of comedy; the trembling narrator, getting the book thrown at him by the overbearing God of Love, shows us, I think, the Chaucerian persona at its absolute best. But behind this humorous conversation exists a variety of literary assumptions that we must extricate and examine carefully, for they indicate the poet's mature concern with issues as important as genre, authorial intent, and the communication of literary meaning to readers in general.

The God of Love opens his remarks with the general accusation that Chaucer has hindered people's devotion to Love:

> ". . . of myn olde servauntes thow mysseyest,
> And hynderest hem with thy translacioun,
> And lettest folk from hire devocioun
> To serve me, and holdest it folye
> To serve Love."
>
> [F 323–27; G 249–53]

Chaucer's "translacioun" of the *Romance of the Rose* has particularly offended the God of Love, probably because Reason's speech in Jean de Meun's section of the work sets forth a spirited analysis of the folly of serving Love.[1] The views in this section of the *Romance of the Rose* certainly confirm the God of Love's observation that "wise folk" have been warned against Love:

> "Thou maist yt nat denye,
> For in pleyn text, withouten nede of glose,
> Thou hast translated the Romaunce of the Rose,
> That is an heresye ayeins my lawe,
> And makest wise folk fro me withdrawe."
>
> [F 327–31, G 253–57]

To indict Chaucer for translating someone else's work is not quite fair, however. Translation was (and is) a service to humanity, regardless of the nature of the work being rendered into a new tongue. Translators should not have to be held accountable for the intentions of their authors; their job is merely to be faithful to the matter they have chosen to treat. Alceste makes this point well:

---

[1] *Romaunt of the Rose*, ll. 4629–5200. There is nothing in Fragment A of this translation (Guillaume de Lorris's section) that would be offensive to the God of Love. Reason's speech occurs in Fragment B, which may not, in fact, be Chaucer's translation but could be the work of an imitator. See Robinson, p. 565.

> "He ne hath nat doon so grevously amys,
> To translaten that olde clerkes writen,
> As thogh that he of malice wolde enditen
> Despit of love, and had himself yt wroght.
>   [F 369–72, G 349–52]

Immunity for its translators is absolutely essential in any culture that wishes to reap the benefits of what "olde bokes" have to offer, for if translators were liable for the crimes of their authors, one can be quite sure that translation would not be attempted at all. Even the rather timid narrator of the Prologue sees the need to articulate this important distinction between author and translator, saying:

> "But trewly I wende, as in this cas,
> Naught have agilt, ne doon to love trespas.
> For-why a trewe man, withouten drede,
> Hath nat to parten with a theves dede."
>   [F 462–65, G 452–55]

This same distinction is applicable to *Troilus and Criseyde* too, though that work is much more nearly the product of Chaucer's own imagination than is his translation of the *Romance of the Rose*. The God of Love's objection to the *Troilus*, like his objection to the *Rose*, is based on material Chaucer took from a source, not on material Chaucer would call his own. What has offended the God of Love, Criseyde's unfaithfulness, is an integral part of Boccaccio's *Filostrato*. About Criseyde, the deity says:

> ". . . of Creseyde thou hast seyd as the lyste,
> That maketh men to wommen lasse triste,
> That ben as trewe as ever was any steel."
>   [F 332–34]

If we are to believe the list of Love's commandments set forth in the *Romance of the Rose* and other court-of-love poems, the

"law" Chaucer challenged when he wrote about Criseyde was
the one that reads "Honor all women," a conventional bit of
courtly "morality" observed by literary artists who were writing
within the strictly defined conventions of the courtly tradition.[2]
But even if one were to categorize *Troilus and Criseyde* as merely
another example of courtly love verse written to promote standard ideas, one would still have to admit that Chaucer is less
guilty of breaking this law than were the authors of his sources,
for not only has his narrator made Criseyde a much more sympathetic character than she was in earlier versions of the tale,
but he also has done everything possible in the *Troilus* to protect her reputation, along with those of all women.[3] In this respect, Chaucer was actually attempting to make his story conform to Love's law, even though the authors of his sources had
not. To accuse him of a "theves dede" is simply not fair.

In the G version of the Prologue, Chaucer expands the God
of Love's remarks into an invective against translators (like
Chaucer himself) who are not careful about choosing what the
God calls "good matere." This issue—the responsibility of the
translator to be selective about what he preserves—gets a full
treatment that deserves our close attention:

> "Hast thow nat mad in Englysh ek the bok
> How that Crisseyde Troylus forsok,
> In shewynge how that wemen han don mis?
> But natheles, answere me now to this,
> Why noldest thow as wel han seyd goodnesse
> Of wemen, as thow hast seyd wikednesse?
> Was there no good matere in thy mynde,
> Ne in alle thy bokes ne coudest thow nat fynde
> Som story of wemen that were goode and trewe?

[2]*Romance of the Rose*, ll. 10403–12. See also Neilson, pp. 169–70, for a collection of the "laws of love" conventionally expressed in "court of love" verse. One
of these laws is that lovers are "to defend and honor" the lady's reputation at
all costs.
[3]See *Troilus and Criseyde* 4.15–21; 5.1093–99, 1771–85. See also C. S. Lewis,
"What Chaucer Really Did to *Il Filostrato*," in *Chaucer Criticism, II: Troilus and
Criseyde and the Minor Poems*, ed. Richard J. Schoeck and Jerome Taylor (South
Bend, Ind.: Univ. of Notre Dame Press, 1961), pp. 25–32.

Yis, God wot, sixty bokes olde and newe
Hast thow thyself, alle ful of storyes grete,
That bothe Romayns and ek Grekes trete
Of sundry wemen, which lyf that they ladde,
And evere an hundred goode ageyn oon badde.
This knoweth God, and alle clerkes eke,
That usen swiche materes for to seke."

[264–79]

This speech advocates a form of censorship based on the assumption that only stories about "good" people can serve as vehicles for moral aims. By implication, the God of Love also
seems to believe that stories about "wicked" people can do
nothing but promote immoral goals. In short, he is confusing
the ethical purpose of a literary work with the traits he per-
ceives in its individual characters, a massive confusion, indeed.
For is it not possible that a narrative concerning a "wicked"
man (to borrow the God of Love's simplistic good/wicked
model) could, in fact, teach ethical truths better than a story
about virtuous characters alone? It all depends on the artist's
control, his "entente" as our narrator puts it. Both *Troilus and
Criseyde* and the *Romaunt of the Rose* were offered to the world
by an artist with absolutely pure intentions:

"Ne a trewe lover oght me not to blame,
Thogh that I speke a fals lovere som shame.
They oghte rather with me for to holde,
For that I of Creseyde wroot or tolde,
Or of the Rose; what so myn auctour mente,
Algate, God woot, yt was myn entente
To forthren trouthe in love and yt cheryce,
And to ben war fro falsnesse and fro vice. . . ."

[F 466–73, G 457–63]

The crime, of course, is the God of Love's. He has badly misread the *Troilus* and the *Romaunt of the Rose*. And in addition to
being confused about the differing responsibilities of authors
and translators, and the distinction between a work's intention

— 77 —

and its characters, the God of Love is unable to see any difference between literature and life. His objection to Chaucer's works is grounded in the notion that people are actually changing their behavior as a result of reading Chaucer's poems. He claims that "wise folk" are withdrawing from service to Love after reading the *Romaunt of the Rose* [F 331, G 257], and that men are beginning to distrust women (the true included) because of Criseyde's unfaithfulness (F 332–34). That is, he alleges that people have construed the *Romaunt of the Rose* and *Troilus and Criseyde* as works of art meant to apply—much too narrowly—to actual human life. They are finding in Chaucer's works simplified morals along the lines of "Love is folly" and "Women are untrue," morals that grossly oversimplify the Chaucerian texts from which they are derived. Instead of viewing these texts as vehicles for philosophical truth, they are seeing them as exempla.[4]

What scholars call the exemplum is, of course, not a well-defined genre. Rather, it seems that what unites narratives we call "exempla" is not any formal or thematic characteristic at all, but a shared desire by their authors (or compilers) that readers interpret them in a certain highly predictable way. J. Th. Welter, the author of the most voluminous study of the

---

[1]That there existed in the medieval period a distinction between works that teach "general knowledge" as opposed to ones intended to affect behavior directly is clear from Averroes's commentary on the *Poetics*, translated in *Classical and Medieval Literary Criticism: Translations and Interpretations*, ed. Alex Preminger, O. B. Hardison, Jr., and Kevin Kerrane (New York: Frederick Ungar, 1974), pp. 349–82. See also Judson Boyce Allen, *The Ethical Poetic of the Later Middle Ages: A Decorum of Convenient Distinction* (Toronto: Univ. of Toronto Press, 1982), esp. pp. 3–66, where the author cites other medieval uses of the distinction. The issues raised by the existence of this distinction and the precise meaning of the terms comprising it are, however, by no means clear. Wesley Trimpi, in "The Ancient Hypothesis of Fiction," *Traditio*, 27 (1971), 1–78, provides much valuable information about the survival—and mutation—of classical theory in the medieval period, especially on the subject of poetry's relationship to philosophy. The reader should also consult O. B. Hardison, Jr., *The Enduring Monument: A Study of the Idea of Praise in Renaissance Literary Theory and Practice* (1962; rpt. Westport, Conn.: Greenwood Press, 1973), pp. 18–67, for documentation of the existence of this relationship through the medieval period and into the Renaissance. The extent to which Chaucer was aware of classical or medieval critical discourse about the distinction between philosophy and exemplary narrative cannot, of course, be determined.

exemplum and the recognized expert on the history of the form, says that the exemplum has three essential features: it is narrative material that is (1) briefly set forth, (2) moralized, and (3) made somehow applicable to the course of daily life.[5] That is, any story can be transformed into an exemplum by the addition of these three features. The exemplum, then, can take many forms and themes, but its intended purpose is to be directly and simply moral, as well as conveniently applicable to its readers' lives. Moralists and teachers kept the exemplum alive throughout the thirteenth and fourteenth centuries, for it allowed them ample room to convey effectively some of the simpler truths upon which Christian doctrine depended. The exemplum could accommodate wide varieties of narrative material as well, since any narrative could be altered or interpreted easily to conform to the needs of a teacher. And for literary historians, the exemplum is fascinating because, as Beryl Smalley and others have shown, it allowed classical literature a special place in Christian pedagogical theory and practice.[6] As we trace the movement of the exemplum through the works of teachers and preachers, we can surely appreciate the extent to which its unequivocal morality and usefulness granted literature (especially pagan literature) an important role in Christian education.

But for writers like Chaucer, who experimented with literature's potential to express philosophical subtleties, irony, and the complexities of life, the widespread presence of heavily moralized exempla must have had serious consequences. First, readers must have become accustomed to seeing moralization, clearly defined characters, and obvious "goods" and "evils" in literature. Furthermore, not finding such things spelled out by

---

[5]*L'Exemplum dans la littérature religieuse et didactique du moyen age* (Paris: Occitania, 1927), p. 3. See also pp. 66–82, 121. Another useful study of the exemplum is Joseph Albert Mosher's *The Exemplum in the Early Religious and Didactic Literature of England* (New York: Columbia Univ. Press, 1911), esp. pp. 1–19. See also G. R. Owst, *Literature and Pulpit in Medieval England*, 2d ed. (1933; rpt. Oxford: Blackwell, 1961), pp. 149–97.

[6]See Beryl Smalley, *English Friars and Antiquity in the Early Fourteenth Century* (Oxford: Basil Blackwell, 1960), esp. pp. 40–45; Owst, pp. 178–79; and Welter, pp. 63–108.

an author, readers might have felt encouraged to supply them on their own. And finally, readers acquainted with classical literature only through exempla might have interpreted all classical narratives as such, since writers of exempla so frequently took stories from antiquity as their subjects.[7] Indeed, reading habits are hard to modify, especially when they are reinforced by the church's own moral authority. The God of Love himself is clearly accustomed to asking only those questions about literature that are suggested by the simplest of exemplary forms. In the G version of the Prologue, for example, he asks the narrator a question that reveals his conception of literature as governed by the exclusive categories of "goodness" and "wickedness":

> "Why noldest thow as wel han seyd goodnesse
> Of wemen, as thow hast seyd wickednesse?"
>
> [268–69]

For him, all literature is exemplary in function; he cannot conceive of literary meaning other than that which might arise from these prerequisite moral categories. Complexity is not expected in literature and hence not found there. The God of Love's judgment of the *Troilus*, then, is that it is an inadequate work of art because it does not offer a "good woman" to serve as a model for readers to trust and emulate.

There are surely few among us who would define Criseyde simply as a character intended to be labeled "bad" by the readers of the poem she lives within. Chaucer has made her a complex woman, as critics and scholars have been quick to point out. Moreover, we all know that the *Troilus* concerns issues that transcend the particularities of Criseyde's changeable heart. And if the *Troilus* is an "example" of love, it is so only in a much more general sense than the God of Love realizes. Although it relates the progress of one couple's love, its message, while concerned with the merits and flaws of the individuals in-

[7]See Smalley, p. 24; Mosher, pp. 55–82; and Welter, pp. 34–62, 83–108.

volved, does not depend upon our sorting the characters into groups of "guilty" or "blameless" ones. Because Chaucer has taken great pains to divide our sympathies between them, the poem finally concerns neither Troilus's nor Criseyde's individual culpability, but rather the consequences of their love in the face of time, fortune, and circumstance. To render harsh judgment upon their behavior or motivation, or to imagine the lovers set in an allegorical world that represents the clash of good and evil such as one might be encouraged to do with an exemplum, is, of course, to simplify and thus to misread the poem's theme, as even its narrator at times seems to do. For the God of Love, "literature" and "exemplum" are merely two names for the same thing, and his sense of the *Troilus*'s meaning is wholly determined by that conflation. In the course of his reading, he has silently supplied the poem with those characteristics deduced from a reading experience limited to works whose moralization is explicit and unequivocal. Such an experience makes him sadly ill equipped to cope with the *Troilus*'s innovations.[8]

It is also not surprising to discover that the God of Love's knowledge of poetic theory is rudimentary. He does not fully understand the function of *translatio*, by means of which a poet's fictions and figures imitate and convey truth to readers. Instead, he subscribes to the inadequate fruit/chaff model, which implies that fictional aspects of a work are wholly expendable and thus finally worthless to whatever didactic purpose the poem might ultimately be intended to contain.[9] The God of Love's most urgent question for the narrator is:

[8]For a clear exposition of how readers bring "generic" knowledge to individual texts, see E. D. Hirsch, Jr.'s discussion of "extrinsic genre" in *Validity in Interpretation* (New Haven: Yale Univ. Press, 1967), pp. 88, 103–06. On the *Troilus*'s generic innovations, see Monica E. McAlpine, *The Genre of Troilus and Criseyde* (Ithaca, N.Y.: Cornell Univ. Press, 1978), esp. pp. 116–20.

[9]For a discussion of the inadequacy of the fruit/chaff model, see David Aers, *Piers Plowman and Christian Allegory* (London: Edward Arnold, 1975), p. 55: "[This model] was so deep-rooted that even when theorists attempted to meet the objections to poetic *figura*, inevitable whenever the shell/kernel model is confronted by responsible criticism . . . , they usually failed to break away from the model which was itself fatal to their cause."

"But yit, I seye, what eyleth the to wryte
The draf of storyes, and forgete the corn?"[10]

[G 311–12]

In a sense, this is a request that the poet abandon precisely those devices that make his art most effective. Reading is not a matter of casting away a work's literal level in order to arrive at its truth. Rather, the truth and the fiction are inseparably joined.

The most significant shortcoming in the God of Love's reading of the *Troilus* is his failure to perceive the poem's complex expression of the relationship between pagan secular love and Christian *caritas*. As we saw in the last chapter, the God of Love assumes that the two kinds of love are identical in their purposes and consequences: he remarks that no true lover will "come in helle" (F 553), that Venus is a "Seynt" (F 338, G 313), and that the pagan ladies whose stories he recommends to the narrator are fine examples of Christian martyrdom in the name of love (G 273–310).[11] In short, his thought is dominated by a rather simple-minded conflation of pagan and Christian love, both of which he sees as illustrations of the same virtue:

"Ek al the world of autours maystow here,
Cristene and hethene, trete of swich matere;
It nedeth nat al day thus for to endite."

[G 308–310]

To view heathens and Christians as believers in the same ethical code is to misrepresent badly the truth that Chaucer so

[10]In the G Prologue, the God of Love says, "Let be the chaf, and writ wel of the corn" (529).

[11]On the incompatibility of Christianity and the "religion of love," see Dodd, pp. 62–63. See also Estrich, "Chaucer's Maturing Art," pp. 334–35, for the observation that Chaucer's God of Love is much more interested in morality of a Christian sort than are love deities in other works, again the result of Chaucer's parodic technique. On the *Troilus*'s complicated juxtaposition of Christian morality and the secular love code, see Alexander J. Denomy, "The Two Moralities of Chaucer's *Troilus and Criseyde*," in *Chaucer Criticism*, ed. Schoeck and Taylor, pp. 147–59.

painstakingly expressed in his *Troilus*—that pagan culture and Christian morality can coexist in a work of art only in a very complicated way. No easy synthesis of the two is possible in an honest estimation of their relationship. In the *Troilus* earthly love is sometimes portrayed as nothing more than vanity, yet at other times we discover that it inspires and sustains a heavenly idealism that Chaucer expresses through the church's own language of devotion. Along with each new situation in the *Troilus* comes a need to define and judge anew its participants' changing relationship to morality and Christian truth, with the remarkable result that Chaucer has written a poem that is faithful to both worlds, the Christian and the pagan alike. He has not falsified either of them by imposing the values of one onto the other; in fact, in the few cases where such imposition occurs in the poem (such as the impatient moral glossing at the end), it is always given voice by the overzealous and unsophisticated narrator, who is decidedly not Chaucer himself. The *Legend*'s God of Love, however, represents the urge to simplify (and thus to falsify) love's relationship to morality. Misreading the general purpose of the *Troilus* is certainly a critical transgression, but a more serious crime is his failure to perceive the poet's distinction between the values of greatly differing cultures and greatly differing kinds of love. The God of Love, however, is probably condemned to everlasting obliviousness of these issues, because he himself is the embodiment of a false synthesis of pagan and Christian values. The character of the God of Love is derived from the assumption, commonly found in conventional literary treatments of love, that human love, whether Christian *caritas* or pagan *eros*, reflects devotion to the same "law."

Because of Chaucer's characteristic refusal to be self-congratulatory, we do not get a "corrected" interpretation of the *Troilus* from the *Legend*'s narrator, even though he is given a chance to respond to the accusations of his deified (and reified) reader. Instead, the only remark we get from him is the reminder that authorial intent ought to be weighed in the literary Last Judgment over which the God of Love presides (F 471–

74, G 461–64). Neither articulate nor forceful, the intimidated narrator only weakly asserts his innocence in response to the charges brought against him. Finally, Alceste is left with the responsibility of defending him, which she does with shrewdness and skill.

First, Alceste reminds the God of Love that many of his opinions on the Chaucerian works he indicts were influenced by the interpretations of his courtiers. She implies that he has a group of hireling readers who work for him, the amatory court's equivalent of commissioned poets in the royal courts on earth, whose duties are to report to the God of Love on the "state of the art" below. And just as there are always corrupt and self-interested poets who flatter kings for profit, there are also corrupt explicators of poetry in the court of the God of Love:

> "This man to yow may falsly ben accused,
> Ther as by right him oughte ben excused.
> For in youre court ys many a losengeour,
> And many a queynte totelere accusour,
> That tabouren in youre eres many a sown,
> Ryght after hire ymagynacioun,
> To have youre daliance, and for envie.
> Thise ben the causes, and I shal not lye.
> Envie ys lavendere of the court alway,
> For she ne parteth, neither nyght ne day,
> Out of the hous of Cesar; thus seith Dante;
> Whoso that gooth, algate she wol nat wante."
> [F 350–61, G 328–39]

Although it may be beneath a god's dignity to spend time reading poems, it is nevertheless bad policy, Alceste remarks, for the God of Love to believe readers whose judgments may be guided by self-interest. He is unfortunately too willing to trust his "losengeours" and their apparently cursory summaries of Chaucer's works. One might argue that since the God of Love's poetic preferences are so obvious to the fawning readers in his retinue, the result is that he "hereth many a tale yfeyned" (G

327) about Chaucer's poetry. Self-interest can (and does) serve as the foundation for readers' literary judgments (let us remember the petty literary quarreling between the Reeve and the Miller in the *Tales*).

The other issues that Alceste raises in defense of the poet are handled carefully and with the kind of deferent tone that any wise lawyer might adopt when arguing her defendant's case before a stern and opinionated judge. Since her past experience with this god has taught her that he "wol nat countrepleted be / In ryght ne wrong" (F 476–77, G 466–67), her case on behalf of the poet must be made without offending her arrogant superior and without appearing to be too prejudiced in favor of Chaucer and his art. She quickly mentions several possible excuses that might persuade the God of Love to lessen the severity of Chaucer's punishment and that might inform him about the difficulties that all poets encounter in the course of their work. Poets not only have sources to deal with, but also the commissions of patrons:

> "And eke, peraunter, for this man ys nyce,
> He myghte doon yt, gessyng no malice,
> But for he useth thynges for to make;
> Hym rekketh noght of what matere he take.
> Or him was boden maken thilke tweye
> Of som persone, and durste yt nat withseye;
> Or him repenteth outrely of this.
> He ne hath doon so grevously amys,
> To translaten that olde clerkes writen,
> As thogh that he of malice wolde enditen
> Despit of love, and had himself yt wroght."
> [F 362–72, G 340–52]

These remarks, intended largely for the benefit of the judge, argue that writing is a complicated process, guided partly by what the past literature of "olde clerkes" has bequeathed and partly by what present audiences demand. True, a commissioned poem might have effects quite different from those in one written independently of a royal command because a poet may be given little or no freedom when he is asked to write laudatory or occasional verse. But commissioned poetry is not necessarily always restrictive; Chaucer's readers need only remember the *Book of the Duchess* to see that a statesman's desire can be carried out imaginatively and freely by a great poet. And with regard to Alceste's remarks on a poet's use of source material, the "thynges for to make," we must remember that all medieval poets depended on past works of literature for the creation of their own. Only poets who, unlike Chaucer, are truly "nyce" would misunderstand the "olde clerkes" of classical antiquity or use their material indiscriminately. Clearly, Alceste's excuses for Chaucer are all fabricated to disguise the fact that Chaucer's heresy against the law of love is probably real, and, more than that, is surely a matter of choice.

Perhaps Alceste's most convincing defense of Chaucer lies in her citation of the poet's juvenilia, especially, she says to the god, the "many an ympne for your halydayes,/That highten balades, roundels, virelayes . . ." (F 422–23, G 410–11). Chaucer was indeed a faithful servant once:

> "The man hath served yow of his konnynge,
> And forthered wel youre lawe with his makynge.
> Whil he was yong, he kepte youre estat;
> I not wher he be now a renegat."
> [G 398–401]

Alceste almost admits here that Chaucer's recent works have entirely ignored the God of Love and his silly "laws." But then, in a brilliantly contrived statement, she points out that all of Chaucer's amatory verse can, if read by "lewed folk," be influential in getting them to pay homage to the God of Love:

> "Al be hit that he kan nat wel endyte,
> Yet hath he maked lewed folk delyte
> To serve yow, in preysinge of your name."
> [F 414–16, G 402–4]

"Learned folk," of course, would never interpret Chaucer's works as exercises designed to get them to "delyte" in serving

Love because they would recognize that Chaucer's love poetry is never solely about love or about how to synthesize it with Christian themes, but is ultimately concerned with other, more significant philosophical matters, for which the subject of love is only the medium.

By the time Alceste finishes with Chaucer's defense, she has ingratiated herself to both parties involved in this confrontation. The narrator, of course, thanks her profusely for cooling the God of Love's ire. And the God of Love himself has learned a lesson or two about poets and their art. But he has learned even more from Alceste's eloquent comments on mercy, justice, and good kingship, the first of which he internalizes so rapidly that, before the Prologue has ended, he tosses off one of Chaucer's favorite lines: "Pite renneth soone in gentil herte" (F 503, G 491). Alceste has managed to teach her arrogant superior about the duties of his office, and she has done this so successfully that, like our narrator, he will "serve alwey the fresshe dayesye" (F 565). As her grateful student, the God of Love says,

> "Madame . . . it is so long agoon
> That I yow knew so charitable and trewe,
> That never yit, syn that the world was newe,
> To me no fond y better noon than yee."
> [F 443–46, G 432–36]

We have no reason to believe, however, that the God of Love could ever attain the virtue, intelligence, or social grace that he lacks in this Prologue, even though he learns some lessons from Alceste. He is there to represent the ineffectual antithesis of Alceste, who, as the elegant and informed mistress of Chaucer's wit, symbolizes his extraordinary art, showing how it can convey, even to kings, the wisdom that is necessary to living a moral life. Chaucer's real worth as a poet, of course, is visible in his poems, which he had written with Alceste's help before this controversy began. But for Alceste to admit proudly that her powers of symbolic representation have helped Chaucer to create his successful works of art would be not only sinful but absolutely out of character. Her modesty, as the Prologue makes clear, is both admirable and sincere:

> Therwith this queene wex reed for shame a lyte,
> Whan she was preysed so in hire presence.
>
> [F 535–36, G 523–24]

Thus in addition to showing Alceste's cleverness in averting the wrath of the people her poet satirizes, Chaucer also describes her unpretentiousness, both qualities of his own verse.

Alceste's full understanding of the God of Love's mind is also visible in her selection of Chaucer's penitential task. Alceste outlines for the God of Love exactly how the poet can, by writing about women's truth in loving, perform poetic restitution:

> ". . . he shal maken, as ye wol devyse,
> Of wommen trewe in lovynge al hire lyve,
> Wherso ye wol, of mayden or of wyve,
> And forthren yow, as muche as he mysseyde
> Or in the Rose or elles in Creseyde."
>
> [F 437–41, G 427–31]

She recognizes here that the God of Love will be easily pleased with any subject matter that manifestly contradicts that of the *Romaunt of the Rose* or any plot that "corrects" the view of women he discerns in his oversimplified reading of Criseyde. Then, a little later, she places further restrictions on the project by assigning Chaucer a genre—the legend—in addition to the subject matter he must follow:

> "Thow shalt, while that thou lyvest, yer by yere,
> The moste partye of thy tyme spende
> In makyng of a glorious legende
> Of goode wymmen, maydenes and wyves,
> That weren trewe in lovyng al hire lyves. . . ."
>
> [F 481–85, G 471–75]

Her choice of the legend as Chaucer's genre is a wise one indeed, given the special circumstances of this penitential exer-

cise. The God of Love can understand and appreciate only simple conflations, however ridiculous, of earthly and heavenly
love because he himself represents such a synthesis, imper-
sonating, as he does, the Christian God. Even obvious distinctions between hagiography and pagan *fabula* are far too subtle
for him to comprehend, so Alceste must ask that Chaucer con-
descend to him by imposing the simple moral patterns of hagiographic exemplary narrative onto the subject matter of the
classical *auctores*. In this way, the God of Love will get his de-
sired synthesis of earth and heaven and thus will have no trou-
ble drawing the facile moral conclusions that his literary experience has led him to seek in narrative art. The God of Love will
like these legends, and he will, we can presume, decide that
they fulfill the requirements of literary art as he defines it.

After Alceste assigns the genre of hagiography to the poet,
she continues to outline for him the ways in which his legends
must conform to the God of Love's literary expectations. They
must tell not only about true women, but also about false men:

> "And telle of false men that hem bytraien,
> That al hir lyf ne do nat but assayen
> How many women they may doon a shame;
> For in youre world that is now holde a game."
> [F 486–89, G 476–79]

Here, Alceste dictates that Chaucer make his narratives directly
applicable to life and thus that he make them conform precisely to the mistaken assumptions the God of Love brought
with him to the *Troilus* and the *Romaunt of the Rose*. The legends
must serve as social correctives by turning women's reputations
from bad to good and by castigating those false men who be-
tray innocent females. The result, of course, can be only distortion and oversimplification, both characteristics of the moral
exemplum in its worst, most limited form.

All along, Alceste has been admirably tolerant of the God of
Love's obtuseness, as troublesome and consequential as it may
be. Yet her patience in the face of such a limited judge should
by no means suggest complicity, for she herself suffers when
the God of Love's reductionist tendencies are turned loose on a

definition of her own identity. To him, she represents a single virtue only, that of a married woman's "fyn lovynge":

> "Why noldest thow han writen of Alceste,
> And laten Criseide ben aslepe and reste?
> For of Alceste shulde thy wrytynge be,
> Syn that thow wost that calandier is she
> Of goodnesse, for she taughte of fyn lovynge,
> And namely of wifhod the lyvynge,
> And alle the boundes that she oughte kepe."
>
> [G 530–36]

But for Chaucer, Alceste has always represented much more than a rigidly contrived archetype of a single theme. Even behind the comic mask of the *Legend*'s narrator, he outlines Alceste's multiple identities, which together make her so rich a symbol:

> "Now knowe I hire. And is this good Alceste,
> The dayesie, and myn owene hertes reste?
> Now fele I weel the goodnesse of this wyf,
> That both aftir hir deth and in hir lyf
> Hir grete bounte doubleth hire renoun.
> Wel hath she quyt me myn affeccioun,
> That I have to hire flour, the dayesye.
> No wonder ys thogh Jove hire stellyfye,
> As telleth Agaton, for hire goodnesse!
> Hire white corowne berith of hyt witnesse;
> For also many vertues hadde shee
> As smale florouns in hire corowne bee."
>
> [F 518–29, G 506–17]

For Chaucer, Alceste is not just a good wife from Thrace, but also a humble English daisy sustained by the light of truth, and a star that brightens the night's darkness. She is, he says, a lady whose virtues are as legion as the petals in her crown. And in addition to those identities, we have seen her take on other roles in this Prologue which further enrich her significance and value to a poet. The pattern of her past life suggests (but does not force on readers) the sacrificial death and resurrection of Christ, her mediation between Chaucer and the God of Love calls up the Virgin Mary's role as arbiter between humanity and an angry God, and her remarks on the correct behavior of rulers show her to be an invaluable source of wisdom for any prince's improvement. As Chaucer's "gide and lady sovereyne" (F 94), Alceste provides the poet with a rich source of subject matter—a pagan story suitable to Christian readers—and with a symbol of the kaleidoscopic variety and fluidity in narrative point of view so characteristic of Chaucer's art. Yet Chaucer does not attempt through her character to unite Christian and pagan perspectives in any unnatural or simplistic way as he does with the God of Love; instead he allows the pagan and Christian sides of Alceste full expression and validity, even when they seem to conflict.

And on the question of useless generic or thematic distinctions, which the *Legend* directly addresses, Alceste's commentary makes clear Chaucer's own views on the subject. In the F version of her famous catalogue of the poet's works, she distinguishes Chaucer's "religious" from his "secular" verse by first naming the secular works and then calling the religious works "other holynesse," a phrase used in part to please the God of Love, but which also indicates her lack of interest in making unprofitable distinctions among the "kinds" of Chaucerian endeavor:

> "He made the book that hight the Hous of Fame,
> And eke the Deeth of Blaunche the Duchesse,
> And the Parlement of Foules, as I gesse,
> And al the love of Palamon and Arcite
> Of Thebes, thogh the storye ys knowen lyte;
> And many an ympne for your halydayes,
> That highten balades, roundels, virelayes;
> And, for to speke of other holynesse,
> He hath in prose translated Boece,
> And maad the lyf also of Seynt Cecile.

He made also, goon ys a gret while,
Origenes upon the Maudeleyne."
[F 417–28]

And in G, she calls the religious poems and translations "other
besynesse" (412), a term that draws even less of a distinction
between the secular and religious works in the catalogue. To
the modern reader, trained to discriminate between "kinds" of
medieval narrative, Alceste's indifference to generic or thematic distinctions may seem troublesome or even shocking. She
sees no reason to distinguish between Chaucer's "Christian"
and "pagan" works, or his "religious" and "secular" efforts,
surely because such broad and useless categories do not come
to terms with the richness of the works themselves and were
not used by the poet when he sat down to write his works. But
Alceste's particular form of synthesis must be distinguished
from the kind the God of Love demands. In the *Troilus*, Christian and pagan viewpoints coexist, not as the God of Love
would have it, by means of a single and therefore limited point
of view, but with one perspective expressed by the story itself
and another by its narrator, who moralizes or "Christianizes" in
a voice external to the story's independent world. Refusing to
"falsifye his mateere," Chaucer can nevertheless juxtapose two
sometimes contradictory but always fully realized points of view
within a single work. This ability to be faithful to his sources
and at the same time distanced from them both in time and in
philosophy is unique to Chaucer and constitutes an honest solution to the problem of how a single poem can preserve classical literature for a Christian world. In the figure of Alceste,
Chaucer embodied his principle of "coexisting perspectives";
through her he shows that such a creative union can be constructed not through sophistry, but through simple truth to
life.

Through the conversation of the narrator, Alceste, and the
God of Love, we are able to see that Chaucer is making an important statement about his *Troilus* and the *Romaunt of the Rose*,
namely, that the proper interpretation of these works requires

intelligence on the part of its readers, not simply the busywork of sorting out the "goods" and "evils" that less complex poetry might demand. The Prologue to the *Legend of Good Women*, then, is far from being a serious palinode to Chaucer's earlier works. Instead of repudiating them, Chaucer is actually defending them, especially the subtle technique of the *Troilus*, by critiquing the habits of reductive readers. However, other poets become the victims of Chaucer's fatal irony, too, because in actually producing the stories in the legendary, Chaucer succeeds in parodying some of the ways in which classical fiction was commonly "modernized" to conform to fourteenth-century tastes. The exemplum form was in vogue during Chaucer's lifetime; one need only recall the lengthy fourteenth-century collections of John Gower (*Confessio Amantis*, for example) or Boccaccio (*De casibus virorum illustrium* and *De claris mulieribus*) to see that the form was popular and taken seriously as art.[12] But aside from the *Legend*, Chaucer never chose to use the exemplum in its purest form, as did many of his contemporaries. He pokes fun at its limitations in the *Monk's Tale*; he borrows features of it for the *Nun's Priest's Tale*; and within the confines of the generically indefinite *Canterbury Tales*, he now and then includes examples of readers turning stories into exempla (let us remember Harry Bailly's moral to the *Shipman's Tale*). Never in his own voice, though, does he present us with what is uncomplicatedly an exemplum. The stories in the *Legend*, then, are unique in being the only true "exemplary" works that Chaucer contributed to the late medieval fashion.

But rather than representing Chaucer's own contribution to this late medieval rage for the moralized classical exemplum, the stories embody the reasons for the poet's disapproval of

[12]On the popularity of the exemplum in the fourteenth century, see John Burrow, *Ricardian Poetry* (London: Routledge and Kegan Paul, 1971), p. 82. Burrow suggests that the scholastic moral philosophy of the previous century may have made medieval poets more aware of literature's utilitarian role and thus might in part explain why exempla were so common. See also John V. Fleming, *The Romance of the Rose: A Study in Allegory and Iconography* (Princeton, N.J.: Princeton Univ. Press, 1969), p. 30, and D. W. Robertson, Jr., *A Preface to Chaucer: Studies in Medieval Perspectives* (Princeton, N.J.: Princeton Univ. Press, 1962), pp. 231–32.

such forms, as the next chapter will show. Not only is it unlike Chaucer to approve of any simpleminded moral clarity (such as that which the "good women" are all meant to project), but it is also uncharacteristic of him to falsify his sources in such a way as to lead a reader into making easy judgments about the classical world, whose people were, to him, more complex than their appearance in moralized narratives could allow. Indeed, taken together, the legends form a powerful attack on unfaithful translators and on the *in bono/in malo* literary critical habits that turned classical texts into imitations of Christian literary works. As Chaucer jokingly demonstrates in the legends, however, at times an artist must submit to an audience's demanding stupidity, for after all, "the world must be served." When they can find classical literature palatable only through the medium of the moralized exemplum, he must let them have it that way. And when they want to see earthly love uncomfortably joined in a literary bond with the saints of the Church, he must let them have a martyrology of love. But it seems that Chaucer got the final word in this little argument between author and reader when he later constructed the *Canterbury Tales*, for there, in the realm where tales meet readers, we usually find that the pilgrim "readers" are the ones deserving correction, not the rich and significant tales that Chaucer provided them to tell.

—4—

Chaucer's Classical Legendary

For as long as the *Legend of Good Women* has been the subject of modern study, critics have found the poem engaging largely because of its Prologue, which includes Chaucer's witty handling of the God of Love and his self-effacing narrator, who is characterized more humorously than any of the poet's previous self-portraits. But few critics have discussed the legends themselves as meaningful Chaucerian works. As even a cursory glance at the *Legend's* relatively short bibliography will show, the bulk of the criticism concerns the Prologue—its relationship to French sources, its subject matter, and its possibly topical origins. But few critics have discussed the legends themselves, and when they have, the discussion has been limited to the diversity of Chaucer's source material and to the ways in which he altered it to conform to the restrictions he was given in the Prologue with regard to plot. Indeed, a common view of the legends, sometimes stated and often implied, is that Chaucer grew tired of the legendary because its subject matter was not his own and because the idea of writing a palinode for the *Troilus* and the *Romaunt of the Rose* (which the Prologue suggests) was sufficiently clear and humorous without the actual task being carried out.

Another problem is that for modern readers the legends are

simply not amusing. After the high comedy of the Prologue, the legends are likely to have the same effect that the Monk's tragedies in the *Canterbury Tales* have on us and the pilgrims: we sigh with relief to see that the storytelling ends before the author's plan has reached completion. To be sure, by the time he gets to his seventh legend, Chaucer himself is telling us how tedious his penance is turning out to be. In the *Philomela*, he acknowledges that his brief treatment of certain elements of the story is the result of boredom alone: "For I am wery of hym for to telle" (2258). And in the *Phyllis*, his impatience with his task is openly admitted:

> But, for I am agroted herebyforn
> To wryte of hem that ben in love forsworn,
> And ek to haste me in my legende,
> (Which to performe God me grace sende!)
> Therfore I passe shortly in this wyse.
>
> [2454–58]

These lines (and others like them) constitute what many critics have seen as evidence that Chaucer was in actuality bored by his legendary and that therefore the only proper response to it is to share the poet's impatience.[1] But this view unfortunately confuses the fictional stance of Chaucer's narrator (who is tired of having to do penance for a ridiculous God of Love) with what Chaucer the poet actually manages to accomplish in his individual legends—despite his narrator's professed boredom and annoyance with the task. To confuse the narrator's attitude toward these narratives with Chaucer's own views about them is, I would argue, as bad a mistake as to confuse the narrator with the poet himself in any other Chaucerian work. The narrator of the *Legend* is indeed bored with having to say the same nice things about the ladies whose stories he is working with—and we, like him, see the foolishness of the project. But the real Chaucer is not wasting time while writing his stories.

[1] See Frank, pp. 189–96, for an excellent summary of this critical view.

Although the legendary is self-consciously "bad art," as a parody it is quite carefully constructed.

First, Chaucer means for us to recognize and appreciate his dextrous (and very funny) avoidance of narrative material that might contradict the legendary's commissioned goal—to tell of "good women." Indeed, the legendary is full of what John Fyler has recently called "the hidden jokes of a translator,"[2] all of which are constructed to show the devastating results of an artist's unfaithful treatment of source material. By certain obvious deletions from his *auctores'* texts, Chaucer is able to show exactly how the literary preferences of the God of Love force the poet to abuse classical works. The censorship advocated by the God of Love makes necessary a massive rewriting of the classics. The comedy here, depending as it does on familiarity with Chaucer's sources, was certainly not lost on the poet's learned contemporaries. Moreover, adding to the comedy he generates by abusing his sources, Chaucer also effectively parodies the exemplum form in his legendary, that form which, he believed, had so inadequately prepared readers for an understanding of his own works.

But in addition to the legendary's broadly comic purposes, its narratives, it should be noted, also raise many serious issues. Like Chaucer's other "comic" works, these legends are complex enough to give the poet space to carry on meaningful deliberation about what he is doing and why. Critics seem not to have noticed what are surely some of Chaucer's reasons for writing these legends to begin with—an interest in clarifying his dislike for certain attitudes among poets and readers toward classical literature, a desire to state with certainty that the subjects of classical poetry are in fact useful to Christian readers even in unrevised form, and a wish to experiment with the medieval practice of "retelling," that complex activity that involves borrowing the "matter" of others to fill a "form" of one's own. This chapter, then, will explore the legends both in the context

[2]*Chaucer and Ovid*, p. 104. See also Goddard, "Chaucer's *Legend of Good Women*, II," pp. 60–86, for a lively commentary on Chaucer's abuse of his sources in the legendary.

of the issues raised in the Prologue and as narratives that to some extent stand alone, able to be read and judged as independent works. Although many of the individual legends merely elaborate cleverly on the understated issues raised in the Prologue, others express new, quite distinct insights into Chaucer's awareness of the problems of translation, the complexities of morality, and the fluidity of form.

Any examination of Chaucer's legends must begin with the God of Love because he is the one whose taste informs the entire project. That he wants exempla from Chaucer's pen is made clear, as we saw in Chapter 3, by his specifications for the legendary's form and purpose. He wants tales about good women, told in a manner that stresses "corn," not "draff" (G 311–12); he expects the stories to apply to people's lives so that they will modify their "sinful" behavior; and he requires the tales to be brief:

> "I wot wel that thou maist nat al yt ryme,
> That swiche lovers diden in hire tyme;
> It were to long to reden and to here.
> Suffiseth me thou make in this manere,
> That thou reherce of al hir lyf the grete,
> After thise olde auctours lysten for to trete.
> For whoso shal so many a storye telle,
> Sey shortly, or he shal to longe dwelle."
>
> [F 570–77]

Much of the comedy of the legendary results directly from Chaucer's straining to meet these particular requirements of the exemplum form. His fulfillment of the God of Love's chosen moral theme is obvious; we get good women and bad men. His attempt to make his narratives mirrors of or commentaries on life is visible in the facile moral applications he appends to all but two of his stories. Seven of the narratives contain passages that try, quite clumsily, to relate the stories to their readers' lives. In *Cleopatra*, for example, Chaucer writes:

> But herkeneth, ye that speken of kyndenesse,
> Ye men that falsly sweren many an oth

> That ye wol deye, if that youre love be wroth,
> Here may ye sen of wemen which a trouthe!
>
> [665–68]

And in *Hypsipyle*, he addresses his audience with the express purpose of drawing connections between contemporary falseness in love and that which is exemplified by Jason:

> But in this hous if any fals lovere be,
> Ryght as hymself now doth, ryght so dide he,
> With feynynge, and with every subtil dede.
>
> [1554–56]

Other direct statements of applicability occur in *Thisbe* (908–11), *Dido* (1254–63), *Lucrece* (1874–85), *Philomela* (2383–93), and *Phyllis* (2559–61). With these remarks, Chaucer the moralist and preacher makes his exempla useful to badly behaved listeners, pointing them to the purpose of his art with clear, unmistakable directions.

With regard to the legends' brevity, the most obvious characteristic of the exemplum, we need only remark that nearly every piece of criticism on these narratives acknowledges their succinctness. Not all critics, however, have seen the legends' brevity as parodic, possibly because the Monk's tragedies, written later for the *Canterbury Tales*, have so improved on the joke that the legends, in comparison, do not seem amusing. Moreover, critics frequently note that brevity is not inherently funny, but is (and was) a valuable device for poets; Robert Worth Frank has successfully described its usefulness to medieval poets in his chapter on the legends' use of *occupatio*, for example.[3] To be sure, Chaucer and other medieval poets often used *brevitas*, *occupatio*, *abbreviatio*, and other related rhetorical devices with serious purpose, to intensify or otherwise stress some point without unnecessary prolixity. These devices were indeed valuable in many contexts, for they enabled an author to suggest richness of detail without dwelling on it, or to elimi-

---

[3] *Chaucer and the Legend of Good Women*, pp. 199–204. See also Fyler, pp. 99–100.

nate parts of a source narrative which might not be relevant to his purpose. Thus in an age whose aesthetic was based in part on the utility and pleasure that could be created by retelling old tales, strategies designed to alter or shorten narrative material were necessary to storytellers, whose purposes and intentions might differ from those of the original authors. Obviously, it is not this general function of *brevitas* that Chaucer parodies in the *Legend*. Rather, he parodies the tendency of writers who through *brevitas* "falsen their matere," with the result that justice is not done to the complexities of morality and character in the original source.

We must not forget that in addition to being commanded to be brief, Chaucer is also asked to follow his "olde auctours" (F 575) in his legends, which means that he is not to depart in noticeable ways from the facts he chooses to narrate from his sources. This restriction, coupled with *brevitas* and the preformed moral conclusion that he is given for his legendary—that women are good—can result only in disaster. *Brevitas* turns into something more like lying, for Chaucer is forced to employ it as a device to mask those details in his sources which would complicate our moral judgments of these women and their deeds and would render the narratives useless as exempla. The legends of Cleopatra and Medea are the most obvious examples of this sort of dishonest selectivity which, as readers have noticed, actually succeeds in transforming these ladies of bad reputation into paragons of goodness. These two legends radically misrepresent their sources largely by means of *abbreviatio*; as scholars have pointed out, opinion in the Middle Ages concerning these women was generally that they were stock examples of satanic lust, unfaithfulness, and other assorted vices; Medea was even considered a murderer.[4] By simple elimination of detail and frequent use of *occupatio*, Chaucer

---

[4]On Cleopatra's medieval reputation, see Beverly Taylor, "The Medieval Cleopatra: The Classical and Medieval Tradition of Chaucer's *Legend of Cleopatra*," *Journal of Mediaeval and Renaissance Studies*, 7 (1977), 249–69. On Medea, see Frank, pp. 83–84; Goddard, pp. 76–77; and Robert K. Root, "Chaucer's *Legend of Medea*," *PMLA*, 24 (1909), 124–53.

can turn the bad into good while creating the illusion of following his "auctours." More destructive, perhaps, are the subtler
effects of *abbreviatio* on the legendary's development of its male
characters. One of Chaucer's most typical editorial practices is
to avoid developing male characters enough to clarify their mo-
tivations for betrayal, and then, by *amplificatio*, to expand on
the women's pitiful states.

I have limited my discussion thus far in this chapter to the
three general characteristics of the exemplum form that
Chaucer parodies in his legendary—its explicit morality, its applicability to life, and its brevity. Chaucer's legendary, however,
is constructed to conform to a particular kind of exemplum,
that is, the saint's life. As a subtype of the exemplum, hagiography usually shares with other exemplary narratives the three
characteristics just mentioned.[5] Its moral purpose is, of course,
beyond dispute; saints' lives were plainly designed to represent
the struggle between good and evil. Despite the great variety of
the individual Christian narratives within it, the genre always
has—at bottom—this purpose.[6] Its applicability to life is also
commonly stressed; from the narrative usually considered to be
the prototype of European saints' legends, Athanasius's *Life of
Anthony*, to the late medieval *specula* containing large numbers
of lives, authors and compilers routinely expressed the useful-

---

[5]Not every saint's life exhibits all three characteristics of the exemplum
form; there are, for example, some very long legends. Moreover, not every legend is intended as a model for behavior; Chaucer's legend of Cecilia is a good
example. But in spite of the exceptions, most saints' legends were considered to
be exempla and were gathered into collections together with other narratives to
form exemplary *specula*. For corroboration of this point, see Mosher, p. 74n.:
"These legendary lives of holy men and women and the Virgin furnished more
exempla than any other class of material. In a sense, a saint's life or a collection
of saints' lives constituted a sort of example-book." Welter, in *L'Exemplum*, also
categorizes saints' lives as exempla, as does Owst, pp. 123–35.

[6]On the struggle between good and evil in saints' legends, see Theodor
Wolpers, *Die Englische Heiligenlegende des Mittelalters* (Tübingen: Max Nie-
meyer, 1964), pp. 28–30. See also Alexandra Hennessey Olsen, "'De Historiis
Sanctorum': A Generic Study of Hagiography," *Genre*, 13 (1980), 415–25;
Charles W. Jones, *Saints' Lives and Chronicles in Early England* (Ithaca, N.Y.:
Cornell Univ. Press, 1947), p. 73; and Rosemary Woolf, "Saints' Lives," in *Con-
tinuations and Beginnings: Studies in Old English Literature*, ed. E. G. Stanley (Lon-
don: Thomas Nelson, 1966), p. 41.

ness of their narratives as models of behavior.[7] Brevity, too, was a common feature of the saints' lives, especially when more than one was collected into a legendary or when a legend appeared with exempla of other kinds to form a compendium.[8]

Another characteristic typical of hagiographical narratives is a claim of historical veracity, a feature that Chaucer mimics in his legendary.[9] In the clearest example, Chaucer writes of Cleopatra's story that "this is storyal soth, it is no fable" (702). However, he also suggests the historicity of other legends by mentioning emperors and kings whose reigns were contemporaneous with the ladies' lives and by having the God of Love in the Prologue talk about classical literary women as if they really existed. The women "in that tyde," the deity remarks, were far truer than men "in this world" (G 302–4). These appeals to history are often comic because of the distortion in some of the narratives of the historical truth. *Cleopatra*, in fact, which includes the strongest assertion of historical validity, is one of the least faithful retellings of a classical source in the entire collection.

The most important feature of Chaucer's legendary, however, is its careless disregard for the differences in subject matter between hagiography and classical literature. The stories in the *Legend* combine pagan erotic love and Christian *caritas* in a facile union that corresponds to the God of Love's own artificial synthesis. As we might expect, the results are appalling,

[7]See Owst, pp. 123–24, 134–35. Indeed, Owst sees imitation as the "chief object" of the saint's life. In Athanasius's *Life of Anthony*, the author twice mentions Anthony's value as a model, once in the Prologue and once in the Conclusion. See also the *Golden Legend*, p. 645: "[The Martyrs] are given to us as models for combat," and Jaroslav Pelikan, *The Growth of Medieval Theology* (600–1300) (Chicago: Univ. of Chicago Press, 1978), p. 125.

[8]See Wolpers, pp. 13, 33; Olsen, p. 411; the *Golden Legend*, p. 687; and Ernst Robert Curtius, *European Literature and the Latin Middle Ages*, trans. Willard R. Trask (1953; rpt. New York: Harper and Row, 1963), p. 160.

[9]On the "historicity" of saints' lives, see Owst, pp. 125–26, where he quotes from a fourteenth-century manuscript as showing this typical claim: "This is no fabull that I sey you." See also Olsen, p. 417; William Nelson, *Fact or Fiction: The Dilemma of the Renaissance Storyteller* (Cambridge, Mass.: Harvard Univ. Press, 1973), pp. 23–24; and Hippolyte Delehaye, *The Legends of the Saints: An Introduction to Hagiography*, trans. V. M. Crawford (1907; rpt. South Bend, Ind.: Univ. of Notre Dame Press, 1961), p. 9, pp. 65–69.

and little justice is done to either of the worlds being represented. Chaucer's classical sources are cheapened by his forcing them into an alien hagiographic pattern,[10] and the spirit of hagiography is profoundly violated by Chaucer's implicit suggestion in these stories that pagan women who die for love are somehow morally comparable to saints dying for the love of God. In fact, in many of the most well-known saint's lives, saints become martyrs by dying at the hands of pagans, that is, *because* of the antipathy between the Christian and pagan cultures. Clearly, in Chaucer's mind, the solution to the problem of how Christian artists should use classical material does not include the wholesale adoption of a hagiographical point of view. The idea of "Cupid's martyrs," the central conception of Chaucer's legendary, is an extreme and finally unworkable one for a serious artist.

To confirm the perversity of this sort of union, even in the opinion of medieval writers who were actively seeking new syntheses of pagan and Christian topics, we need only to turn to Boccaccio, whose *De claris mulieribus* is quite probably one of Chaucer's medieval sources. Boccaccio did not include any Christian saints in his collection because he did not think they were appropriate in the company of pagans. In his preface he writes, "It seemed that they could not very well be placed side by side and that they did not strive for the same goal."[11] To Boccaccio, the natural virtue of pagans is somehow different from Christian virtue, and the two must not be confused, or even combined in the same exemplary collection. Furthermore, he reminds us that the virtues of Christian saints had already been described in books reserved for them alone:

> . . . not only do Christian women, resplendent in the true, eternal light, live on, illustrious in their deserved immortality, but we

---

[10]On the single "pattern" of Christ's life as it is demonstrated in saints' lives, see Olsen, p. 411, who reminds us of Gregory of Tours's comment: "And it is asked by many whether we should say the Life of the saints, or the Lives." See also Pelikan, p. 174.

[11]*Concerning Famous Women*, trans. Guido A. Guarino (New Brunswick, N.J.: Rutgers Univ. Press, 1963), p. xxxviii.

know that their virginity, purity, saintliness, and invincible firmness in overcoming carnal desire and the punishments of tyrants have been described in special books, as their merits required.[12]

Though the lives of the saints may have been the generic inspiration for Boccaccio's collection of exempla, he is nevertheless careful to draw a distinction between his own work and the "special books" devoted to saints. To him, saints and classical women were simply not alike.[13]

Although Chaucer's comic project in the *Legend* is different from Boccaccio's serious one in *De claris mulieribus*, the two authors were faced with the same problem—how to retell the lives of classical women in such a way as to make them useful to Christian readers as "examples" of behavior. Boccaccio's solution to this problem was to tell, quite plainly, the stories of natural virtue to be found in classical texts. He did not attempt to introduce the conceptions of hagiography into his collection, beyond the simple idea of making his stories roughly conform—in imitative purpose—to the numerous collections of the lives of female saints. But Chaucer's project is much more difficult, because he has to ignore the incompatibility of the two narrative types in making saints out of classical women, including classical women who were enthralled in what is, from a Christian point of view, an unredeeming passion.

Only Chaucer's *Legend of Lucrece* is, in some ways, an exceptional case. The poet did not have to alter its plot much, because Lucretia was, quite literally, a martyr for chastity, exhibiting (though only superficially, as we shall see) the same virtue that we find in so many female saints. Lucretia may have been, in fact, the most "canonical" of Chaucer's ladies, having survived, good reputation intact, the scrutiny of Jerome and other Christian authorities.[14] But for Augustine, whom Chaucer's

---

[12]*Concerning Famous Women*, p. xxxix.

[13]Boccaccio's translator, Guido A. Guarino, writes: "He did not write of saints and martyrs simply because he was not drawn to them, while classical antiquity held him enthralled with its charms" (*Concerning Famous Women*, p. xxv). The issue is probably more complicated than Guarino suggests.

[14]For Jerome's approval of her, see *Adversus Jovinianum* 1.46 (*PL* 23, col. 287). Also see Odo of Cluny's *Collationum libri tres*, *PL* 133, col. 557. For exam-

narrator unwisely names in his opening lines, Lucretia's "virtue" was actually a crime, for in killing herself, she was killing an innocent victim. As for the motive behind her suicide, Augustine remarks that it was obviously not the "love of purity," but the "overwhelming burden of her shame." Thus, he concludes, there is a significant difference between the "true sanctity" of Christian martyrs and the illusory virtue of Lucretia.[15] This problem raised by Augustine does not interfere with Chaucer's enterprise, however. The narrator simply ignores the substance of Augustine's lengthy commentary on Lucretia's case and attributes to him a feeling of "gret compassioun" (1690) for her. He then introduces a theme common to hagiography—commemoration—by remarking that his story is being told "to preyse and drawe to memorye" (1685) the event in her life which resulted in her "martyrdom."[16]

Chaucer's handling of Lucrece's rape and subsequent death is reminiscent of hagiography in other ways as well. One of his only additions to this story's plot is Lucrece's swoon, which occurs during her rape, and which Chaucer describes as deep and deathlike:

> She loste bothe at ones wit and breth,
> And in a swogh she lay, and wex so ded,
> Men myghte smyten of hire arm or hed;
> She feleth no thyng, neyther foul ne fayr.
> [1815–18]

Lucrece's swoon serves several purposes. First, it renders her oblivious to Tarquin's violence, sparing her the conscious expe-

---

ples of the medieval view of Lucretia's story, see *Gesta Romanorum*, trans. Charles Swan and revised by Wynnard Hooper (London: Bohn's Antiquarian Library, 1891), p. 239; *Le Ménagier de Paris*, trans. Eileen Power (London: Routledge and Sons, 1928), pp. 101–5; and the *Romance of the Rose*, ll. 8608ff. Some of Chaucer's alterations of the original story are discussed by Frank, pp. 93–110, and by Edgar Finley Shannon, *Chaucer and the Roman Poets* (Cambridge, Mass.: Harvard Univ. Press, 1929), pp. 220–28.

[15]*The City of God* 1.19. See also John S. P. Tatlock, "Chaucer and the *Legenda Aurea*," *MLN*, 45 (1930), 296–98.

[16]See Owst, pp. 123, 125–56, who quotes two typical examples of hagiography being called a means of "blessid commemoraciouns" and a form of "remembrance."

rience of (and, of course, complicity in) such an outrage. It is intended, perhaps, to resemble the otherworldly states in which God allows His beloved saints miraculously to endure physical suffering (in fires that do not burn them, in hot baths that do not scorch, etc.).[17] Second, it worsens Tarquin's character since it suggests to us that his desire for Lucrece has, as its object, what is most "lifeless" about her—her mere physical form. And third, it is a primitive example of the typological structure sometimes used in hagiographic narratives in that it "prefigures" Lucrece's real death.[18]

Finally, Lucrece's story is fairly easy to force into the hagiographical mold since her own compatriots venerated her for her virtue; as Chaucer writes, she was "holden there/A seynt, and ever hir day yhalwed dere" (1870–71). With these lines, the narrator slyly introduces the terminology he needs to make the Christian parallel clear. Moreover, her corpse, carried through the streets to give witness to the spreading story of her "martyrdom," is surely meant to recall the relics of a Christian saint, circulated with a legend, so that men "may see and here" (1867) of miraculous forebearance and power in the face of great suffering.

These hagiographic devices in Lucrece's tale, coupled with the digression (1759–74) that makes Tarquin fully equal in lustful power to the sexually obsessed pursuers of female saints,[19] by no means confer upon her any easy canonization, however. As hard as our narrator may work to make Lucrece fit the mold of a chaste Christian, she is still saintly only by the standards of her own pagan culture, dying, as Augustine says, not for Christian truth but through shame over the result of someone's violent and lustful desire. Tarquin's character, too, is odd in the extreme, for Chaucer has permitted him to display the tender

[17]See, for example, the *Golden Legend*, pp. 593, 632, 695; and *The South English Legendary* 1, ed. Charlotte D'Evelyn and Anna Mill, EETS e.s. (London: Oxford Univ. Press, 1956), pp. 63–64, ll. 41–45, 56–60.

[18]Compare, for example, the "foreshadowings" of death in the life of St. Martha, *Golden Legend*, p. 393.

[19]See, for example, the *Golden Legend*, pp. 52, 540, 552, 571; and *The South English Legendary* 1, p. 19, ll. 8–16; p. 293, ll. 43–50; and 2, p. 586, ll. 5–8.

longings of a stricken courtly lover, even though these details do not fit the purpose of hagiographic legend. The lustful pursuers of female saints should never be allowed to show poignant emotion; such a display conflicts with the moral clarity that such tales are designed to convey. Thus Chaucer's attempt to equate Lucrece's life with that of a saint results in an obviously contrived piece of literary deception that violates the generic specifications of both hagiography and courtly narrative. The story also violates its own professed interest in the strict correlation of "word" and "dede" (1706–7), "contenaunce" and "herte" (1738–39). Chaucer's praise of Lucrece for having beauty "by no craft . . . feyned" (1749) does not seem to deter him from feigning the beauty of sainthood for her. And finally, if we can trust Chaucer's words in the Prologue to his own life of St. Cecilia, the writing of saints' lives is in part a valid method of preventing idleness, a sin with which the tale of Lucrece is concerned. Both Lucrece and Chaucer work to deter that sin; she spins, while he writes. But one must finally question the validity of Chaucer's labor here, for it can hardly be described as "leveful bisynesse," as the Second Nun describes it. He certainly meant for us to notice Lucrece's simple but productive task and to contrast it with his own more complex, more directly "Christian" one which is, however, ultimately idleness.

Another legend that betrays Chaucer's hagiographic adjustments is the *Legend of Cleopatra*. He easily conveys her "truth in love" and other virtues by simply suppressing the historical facts of her seduction and manipulation of Antony and by ignoring her unseemly political life. Her qualifications for "sainthood" are more difficult to establish, though, and Chaucer finally has to alter several details of her biography to make her life conform to a hagiographical pattern. Chaucer's most original contribution to the story of Cleopatra is, of course, his rendering of her death. In all of the poet's sources, Cleopatra's suicide was the result of her placing an adder at her breast, but in Chaucer's version of her story, she dies in a snake pit, a radical departure from tradition and one whose purpose is not immediately apparent. Yet if one recalls that saints' lives often display reenactments of the life of their figural leader Christ, then one can profitably interpret Cleopatra's descent into the snake pit as an event intended to echo one of the most important incidents from the life of Christ, his descent into hell. Similarly, this event recapitulates Alceste's own descent into the underworld. She is to be seen, of course, as the model for the lives of other classical ladies (F 542, G 532), a notion that the narrator of the legendary takes literally as he constructs his martyrology of love.

Cleopatra's life, like Christ's and Alceste's, has a self-sacrificial theme, but not, in its original version, a trip into hell. To make up for this inadequacy, Chaucer creates a miniature snake-filled "underworld" to receive his heroine so that her life can approximate—at least in a general way—the prototypical lives of her figural models.[20] Unfortunately, however, this clever imitation of hagiographical patterning does not make Cleopatra any more saintlike than her original story did, for though she now descends into hell, it is a hell she painstakingly constructs for herself. In digging her snake pit, Cleopatra seems almost aware that her damnation is self-imposed:

> Among the serpents in the pit she sterte,
> And there she ches to have hire buryinge.
> Anon the nadderes gonne hire for to stynge,
> And she hire deth receyveth with good cheere,
> For love of Antony that was hire so dere.
>
> [697–701]

We have here only a poor imitation of a saint. Cleopatra willingly undergoes torture and martyrdom, yet instead of having them thrust upon her, she willfully chooses them as her fate, proving only that she is her own persecutor. Not able to approximate the true tragedy of Christ's and Alceste's self-sacrifice, descent, and subsequent resurrection, Cleopatra remains

---

[20]John S. P. Tatlock, "Notes on Chaucer: Earlier or Minor Poems," *MLN*, 29 (1914), 99n, also speculates on this snake pit and its relationship to Hell.

in the snake-filled hell of her own devising, dying not for a noble cause, but, instead, in vain. This legend, the shortest and most elliptical of all, is perhaps Chaucer's best statement about the vanity of his task. Though this pagan life can be supplied with formal correspondences to Christian patterns, ultimately the relationship remains superficial. Even the expensive "shrine" Cleopatra creates to keep Antony's sacred memory alive among the Egyptians is an empty mockery of the precious jewel-studded reliquaries for the remains of saints.[21] Cleopatra's pathetic attempt to canonize Antony resembles Chaucer's own efforts to adorn his worldly tales with the superficial glitter of holy rhetoric or to make them conform to sacred plots.

The unfinished *Hypermnestra* shares with *Cleopatra* several incidents that schematically retrace Alceste's exemplary life—love for a husband, self-sacrifice in order to save him, and descent into "hell." Hypermnestra's fatal act was to disobey her father's command by sparing the life of her husband Lynceus. As a result of this noble deed, she is caught and "fetered in prysoun," where, the narrator wants us to believe, she eventually dies. If the fetters and the prison are meant to suggest the confinement of souls in hell, then Hypermnestra is reliving the tragedy of Alceste. She is destined to be a "sacrifice" from the moment she is married; indeed, Chaucer's description of her wedding festivities (which departs from all of his sources) is frightening rather than joyful in its detail:

> The torches brennen, and the laumpes bryghte;
> The sacryfices ben ful redy dighte;
> Th'encens out of the fyre reketh sote;
> The flour, the lef is rent up by the rote
> To maken garlondes and crounes hye.
> [2610–14]

The burning torches, the fire, the "sacryfices," and the uprooted flowers all suggest the hell Hypermnestra was destined to occupy.

[21]The analogy of the reliquary may have been intended by Chaucer. In *The Sacred Shrine*, Hirn observes that it was a common practice in the late medieval

— 109 —

But Hypermnestra's destiny, her puppetlike existence which is controlled by the stars, is also exactly what makes her unlike Alceste. In this story, Chaucer's major departure from his sources is his addition of detailed astrological lore.[22] Hypermnestra is given beauty by Venus, "trouthe" by Jupiter, and her visit to prison by Saturn. Her whole character is molded from above:

> The Wirdes, that we clepen Destine,
> Hath shapen hire that she mot nedes be
> Pyëtous, sad, wis, and trewe as stel,
> As to these wemen it acordeth wel.
>
> [2580–83]

In other words, Hypermnestra's heroic act of charity is really not her own choice at all. Both her self-sacrifice and her punishment were written in the stars, and she merely acted out the tragic role that was forced upon her. This fact makes her less morally admirable than Alceste, who chose to die without the help of any astrological planning, making her decision truly charitable and worthy of reward. Had Hypermnestra been the author of her own destiny as was Alceste, then, in Chaucer's own words, "of the shef she sholde be the corn" (2579). But like the uprooted flowers at the wedding feast, she withers before she can bear fruit.

Even though Chaucer's story is incomplete, it is clear that he did not intend to end it with less tragedy than any of the other legends. Hypermnestra's husband leaves the court without her, and the tale comes to an abrupt halt just as she is locked in

---

period "to use heathen works of art as coverings for Christian relics. Crusaders and pilgrims brought with them relics lying in costly cases and receptacles which they had procured in the East. . . . The same liberality was shown with regard to the profane art of the European nations. As the Church on the whole rejected nothing—whether old folk legends or heathen customs or motives or artistic decoration—so too it gave house-room to gems, receptacles, and implements. Worldly objects were transformed into holy shrines" (p. 53).

[22]Hypermnestra's nativity is described by Frank, pp. 160–61, and Fyler, p. 107, who has a view very similar to mine of this legend's irony.

prison. Closely following Ovid's account in the *Heroides*, Chaucer chooses not to lighten Hypermnestra's grief or mention her later reward, as does Boccaccio in *De claris mulieribus*, in which she becomes Lynceus's queen after the wicked Danaus is killed. Chaucer is thus able to maintain some resemblance between this plot and that of Alceste's tragic biography—without, of course, the triumphant resurrection that distinguishes Alceste from the "saints" that imitate her. But as in *Cleopatra*, Chaucer finally shows us that the heroine only superficially approximates the virtue of Alceste. The implication, again, is that recording only the misleading and artificial resemblances between two very different human lives does little justice to the complexity of either. In order to force Hypermnestra into Alceste's mold, her life must be radically simplified, emptied of articulate motives, and, with the worst insult of all, deprived of a happy ending.

These first three legends I have discussed overtly display Chaucer's crafty reshaping of classical fiction to fit the moral hagiographic form that the God of Love will like and deem superior to any other possible forms that these ladies' stories can take.[23] In so doing Chaucer suppresses parts of the ladies' lives to make them more virtuous and alters their biographies to fit the preconceived shape of Alceste's prototypical life. But Chaucer tells us in other ways both that he is painfully aware of the literary assumptions that his penance must reflect and that he is conscious of the processes necessary to this task. For example, several passages in the legendary, particularly in the *Legend of Philomela* and the *Legend of Medea*, reveal that Chaucer is aware of his manipulation of "matter" and "form."

Chaucer opens the story of Philomela with some lines addressed to God who, as "yevere of the formes," carried in his mind the "idea" of the world before he undertook its actual construction:

---

[23]Delehaye notes that hagiographers commonly altered their sources or added to them in order to make their heroes and heroines appear in the best light possible. See *Legends of the Saints*, pp. 68–69. Some of Chaucer's methods in the *Legend* are comparable.

Thow yevere of the formes, that hast wrought
This fayre world, and bar it in thy thought
Eternaly, er thow thy werk began. . . .

[2228–30]

Karl Young has suggested that Chaucer derived these opening lines from one of the many *accessus* that were so often added to Ovid's works in the Middle Ages as "critical introductions" to aid the reader in his quest for moral edification.[24] But this passage about the giver of forms also describes the task of the human creator, the artist who must hold within his mind, as Geoffrey of Vinsauf relates, the plan of his "edifice" before he carries out its construction.[25] Quoted by Pandarus in *Troilus and Criseyde*, this metaphor succinctly expresses the care with which any artist must plan the project he has chosen; from the beginning, he must have mental control over the varied details that will make up his finished product.

Philomela herself vividly enacts the role of the giver of forms in this legend. After Tereus cuts out her tongue to prevent her from spreading the story of his violent deeds, she weaves her tragedy into a tapestry to tell what actually happened. And though this truth must be told indirectly, Philomela's translation of it does not appear to have diminished its horror, for Procne, when seeing it, "no word she spak, for sorwe and ek for rage" (2374). Here, truth clearly finds effective expression in art. In fact, one might judge Philomela a much better "translator" than Chaucer himself in this legendary, for she is weaving true experience into art without the kind of falsification Chaucer uses in giving form to his ladies' lives. Yet her skill as a narrative artist cannot, of course, make her a Christian saint. She, like the other ladies, still falls short of fulfilling the requirements of a perfectly realized Christian life.

[24]Chaucer's Appeal to the Platonic Deity," *Speculum*, 19 (1944), 1–13. On the *accessus* tradition, see Edwin A. Quain, "The Medieval *Accessus ad Auctores*," *Traditio*, 3 (1945), 215–64. For typical *accessus*, see those written by Bernard of Utrecht and Conrad of Hirsau which have been edited by R. B. C. Huygens, *Accessus ad Auctores* (Leiden: E. J. Brill, 1970).

[25]*Poetria nova* 40–48 and *Troilus and Criseyde* 1.1065–69.

The *Legend of Medea*, like the *Philomela*, also defines its heroine as a "giver of forms." Only two lines into her narrative, Chaucer writes:

> As mater apetiteth forme alwey,
> And from forme into forme it passen may,
> Or as a welle that were botomles,
> Ryght so can false Jason have no pes.[26]
>
> [1582–85]

Written in reference to Jason's insatiable desire, these lines suggest that he searches insistently for something to lend form to his base longings, just as the chaotic "matter" of the medieval philosophers constantly "apetiteth" new existence.[27] In literary terms, this passage reminds us that the basic stories of history and past fiction may pass from "forme into forme"; they are not limited to a single, inviolable shape. But the irony here is that Jason's indiscriminate shape changing constitutes little more than deception. Both Hypsipyle and Medea become the unfortunate victims of Jason's endless quest for "form." He is an experienced deceiver who, by "the art and craft" (1607) of love, leads the innocent into believing that his "farced" words are true. Like the fowler of Chaucer's Prologue (F 130–39, G 118–26), Jason is a master of sophistry. He is the legendary's

[26]These lines are from Guido delle Colonna's *Historia Destructionis Troiae*, the modern edition edited and translated by Nathaniel E. Griffin, Medieval Academy of America Publication 26 (Cambridge, Mass.: Mediaeval Academy, 1936), p. 17.

[27]For a short history of the philosophy of matter and form, see Leff, pp. 49, 70, 118, 120–23, 152–64, 185–89, 193, 211, 217. Before Aquinas, medieval thinkers in general believed that form gave being to substance and was closely connected to the "ideas" that lay in God's mind. Our knowledge of things derived ultimately from our observations of these "forms." Matter itself was recalcitrant and confused and could not exist without a "form" in which to be contained. Aquinas's revision of this Platonic scheme was to allow matter a more independent and important place in theories of existence. To Aquinas, matter was a "principle of individuation" by which things were made distinct from one another. On the early application of these ideas to rhetorical theory, see Boethius's *De differentiis topicis* 4, cited in John O. Ward's "From Antiquity to the Renaissance: Glosses and Commentaries on Cicero's *Rhetorica*," in *Medieval Eloquence*, ed. James J. Murphy (Berkeley: Univ. of California Press, 1978), p. 43–44, 50.

example of a lying poet, whose fictions ensnare those who attend to them. Appropriately, he is compared twice to a wily hunter:

> For evere as tendre a capoun et the fox,
> Thow he be fals and hath the foul betrayed,
> As shal the good-man that therfore hath payed.
>
> [1389–91]

> Thow madest thy recleymyng and thy lures
> To ladyes of thy statly aparaunce,
> And of thy wordes, farced with plesaunce,
> And of thy feyned trouthe and thy manere,
> With thyn obeÿsaunce and humble cheere,
> And with thy contrefeted peyne and wo.
>
> [1371–76]

Jason's trickery is possible because of his verbal skills and his ability to counterfeit the truth. In one of Chaucer's original passages in *Hypsipyle*, we find Jason and Hercules acting as coconspirators in the creation of a fiction intended to "bedote" Hypsipyle into marriage:

> This Ercules hath so this Jason preysed
> That to the sonne he hath hym up areysed,
> That half so trewe a man there nas of love
> Under the cope of heven that is above;
> And he was wis, hardy, secre, and ryche.
>
> [1524–28]

It is just this kind of dissemblance that causes both Hypsipyle and Medea to fall victim to the beastly desires of the man who pursues them. They are moved by the fictions they too easily believe, especially the false representations of Jason's character which make any accurate judgment of him impossible. It would not be far from the truth to say that Chaucer's role as "misrepresenter" in this legendary is much like that of the deceitful Jason. Both use their artistry to distort complex human characters into mere blueprints of "goodness" and "faithfulness" in love. Just as Jason profits from the innocence of these credulous women, moving from them to "yit the thridde wif anon" (1660), so too Chaucer exploits these ladies (and the men) by regarding their lives as disorderly matter on which to impose his own prearranged form. Considerably simplified in Chaucer's versions, each of these ladies' lives is deprived of any distinctive detail that could make them more than simply items in the list of "good women" they now comprise. Chaucer, the bad translator, has done to all these women what Jason did to Hypsipyle—he "tok of hir substaunce/What so hym leste, unto his purveyaunce" (1560–61).

In *Ariadne*, Chaucer again modifies the details of his sources to emphasize similarities, as a saint's life might, between his characters and exemplary models. This time, however, the males are the center of attention as Chaucer strives to show parallels between the experience of Theseus, who escapes the labyrinth, and that of Admetus (Alceste's husband), who is saved from death and eternal confinement in the underworld. Aiding Chaucer in this task was a medieval tradition in which the story of Theseus's adventures in Crete was allegorically interpreted as a Christian's escape from damnation and the jaws of the fiend. The opening line of *Ariadne*, "Juge infernal, Mynos, of Crete kyng" (1886), follows Boccaccio in assigning to Minos the role of judge of the lower world, thus implicating him in the drama of Theseus's struggle against potential damnation.[28] But Chaucer further strengthens the comparison of the labyrinth and the underworld by describing Theseus as damned (1953, 2030), the labyrinth as a "prysoun, ther he shal descende" (1997), and most appropriately, the Minotaur as the "fend" (1996), this last detail suggesting an allegory in keeping with Pierre Bersuire's interpretation of the Minotaur as, among other things, "*diabolum.*"[29]

[28]See Robinson, p. 851n.
[29]See Pierre Bersuire's *Reductium Morale* 15, reprinted as *Metamorphosis Ovidiana Moraliter . . . Explanata*, 1509; facsim., intro. Stephen Orgel (New York: Garland, 1979), 8.63. Also see *Gesta Romanorum* 63, p. 112, which tells essentially the same story, interpreting the beast as the devil.

Chaucer, of course, does not intend his narrative to be allegorized in any way. He includes these details merely to underscore the parallels between Ariadne and Alceste, both of whom can now be viewed as saviors, since their actions preserve men from the perils of hell. In most medieval tellings of this story, Theseus escapes the labyrinth and kills the Minotaur with the aid of Dedalus, who, as maker of the maze, suggests the string and the wax as a means of escaping it.[30] In Chaucer's version, however, Dedalus is not even mentioned by name, and his role as keeper of the maze is replaced with a nameless "gaylor," whose function in the story is minimal. In Chaucer's telling, it is Ariadne who takes pity on Theseus and with the aid of her sister Phedra explains to him the best means of escape:

> And by the techynge of this Adryane
> He overcom this beste, and was his bane;
> And out he cometh by the clewe agayn
> Ful prively, whan he this beste hath slayn.
>
> [2146–49]

Furthermore, Ariadne's crown, later made part of a constellation, serves conveniently as an imitation of Alceste's crown of martyrdom and complete stellification. We have in Ariadne, then, another lesser Alceste.

As in many of the other legends, however, the heroine's misfortunes are in some ways ironic. The labyrinth, conventionally a metaphor for the intricacies of art,[31] may have brought

[30]Sanford Brown Meech, in "Chaucer and an Italian Translation of the *Heroides*," *PMLA*, 40 (1930), 110–28, points out that most medieval and some classical discussions of this story name Dedalus as Theseus's helper. Ovid, in the *Heroides*, is the exception.

[31]On the image of the labyrinth and its relation to art, see Frank, p. 132. See also Donald R. Howard, *The Idea of the Canterbury Tales* (Berkeley: Univ. of California Press, 1976), pp. 326–32, where the figure of the labyrinth is discussed as it appears in Chaucer's other works. It is also possible that the title of Eberhard the German's art of poetry, *Laborintus*, suggests this connection. And finally, in the fifteenth century, Gavin Douglas suggests this connection in his Prologue to the third book of the *Aeneid*, ed. David F. C. Coldwell, Scottish Text Society, no. 25 (Edinburgh: Blackwood and Sons, 1957), ll. 10–16. Perhaps the connection between the labyrinth and art was implied in the word *involucrum*, the term most frequently used by mythographers and others to de-

about the salvation of Theseus, but for poor Ariadne, its halls seem to symbolize the lies that caused her undoing. Misled by Theseus's false promises and the hidden snares of his artful love talk, Ariadne ends up alone on a wilderness island, inhabited, like the labyrinth, with "bestes wilde." Wondering which way to go, she wanders about, painfully realizing that her former ability to give advice on how to escape tricky snares is now gone:

> "Allas! where shal I, wreche wight, become?
> For thogh so be that ship or boot here come,
> Hom to my contre dar I nat for drede.
> I can myselven in this cas nat rede."
>
> [2214–17]

Now in her own labyrinth, Ariadne must be rescued through someone else's compassion, just as Theseus was rescued by her own:

> The goddes han hire holpen for pite,
> And in the signe of Taurus men may se
> The stones of hire corone shyne clere.
>
> [2222–24][32]

Thus in *Ariadne*, as in other legends, we can see images, phrases, allusions to Alceste, and other embellishments that are

---

scribe the enigmas of myth and fable, especially those fables whose meaning is deliberately concealed by their authors. On the term *involucrum* see Brian Stock, *Myth and Science in the Twelfth Century: A Study of Bernard Silvester* (Princeton, N.J.: Princeton Univ. Press, 1972), pp. 48–62. Also see M.-D. Chenu, *"Involucrum:* Le mythe selon les théologiens médiévaux," *AHDLMA,* 22 (1956), 75–79, and H. Brinkmann, "Verhüllung *(Integumentum)* als literarische Darstellungsform im Mittelalter," *Miscellanea Medievalia* 8, *Der Begriff der Repraesentatio im Mittelalter* (Berlin, 1971), pp. 314–39. Finally, Boccaccio's labyrinth, the labyrinth of love in his *Corbaccio,* trans. Anthony K. Cassell (Urbana: Univ. of Illinois Press, 1975), pp. 6, 7, 10, 14, may be useful in the interpretation of Chaucer's *Ariadne.*

[32]Ariadne's crown is mentioned in Bernard Silvester's *De Mundi Universitate* (see Wetherbee's translation, p. 77), as well as in several other classical and medieval works, including Dante's *Paradiso* (13.1–30). See *TLL,* s.v. *corona,* 3.B.2.b, for citations.

designed to call attention to the poet's self-reflexive "making."

In this legendary, which has as one of its purposes the con-
demnation of men as one-sided villains in matters of love, the
Legend of Thisbe, our next subject, comes as a surprise. It is an
unusual choice for inclusion in a collection of stories intended
to extol women's constancy and virtue in the face of men's de-
ceits. This story differs markedly from the other narratives in
the *Legend* in that it concerns the tragic deaths of two faithful
lovers instead of just one, both of whom die for their love. Furthermore, the story does not contribute much to the legendary's hagiographical scheme because Thisbe's experiences are
not made to conform to Alceste's, nor is Pyramus drawn in
such a way as to remind us of Admetus's own close escape from
death. And finally, Thisbe's name is not often included among
standard medieval catalogues of exemplary female sufferers.
Though her story was told with as much frequency as the others, she does not seem to be a regular member of conventional
lists designed to memorialize the names of classical women who
suffered in love. Unlike Cleopatra, Dido, Hypsipyle, Medea,
Lucretia, Ariadne, Philomela, Phyllis, and Hypermnestra,
Thisbe is not an automatic candidate for commemoration, because she does not illustrate the premise that women are more
frequently victimized by their partners than are men. In fact,
Chaucer has to moralize this narrative awkwardly after he has
told it, in hopes of making it appropriate to his project. First,
Thisbe herself is given a clumsy death speech, meant to help
her turn her particular misfortune into an exemplum of universal female worthiness, a speech that ends by suggesting that
the sole reason for her suicide is to further women's reputations as true lovers:

> "But God forbede but a woman can
> Ben as trewe in lovynge as a man!
> And for my part, I shal anon it kythe."
> [910–12]

Second, the narrator concludes his version of the story by
pointing out once again that Thisbe has competed well with

any virtuous man: "A woman dar and can as wel as he " (923).
These strained moralizations help make Thisbe's story com-
ply with the formulaic theme Chaucer is seeking to convey in
this legendary. Still, this story describes an exceptionally virtuous man, one who dies perhaps more nobly and for a better
reason than Thisbe. Chaucer does not alter his portrait of
Pyramus to make him diabolical, as he does many of the other
male portraits in his legendary, and he does little to suppress
Pyramus's central importance in this narrative. In fact, he calls
attention to his virtue in the following lines:

> Of trewe men I fynde but fewe mo
> In alle my bokes, save this Piramus,
> And therfore have I spoken of hym thus.
> For it is deynte to us men to fynde
> A man that can in love been trewe and kynde.
>
> [917-21]

Clearly, Pyramus stands nearly alone as an example of mascu-
line truth in love. Though such are few, however, readers familiar with Chaucer's own corpus would immediately think of
another, equally true man—Troilus, whom Chaucer extolled
earlier in his career as a man deserving poetic treatment because of his steadfast (and tragic) love. In fact, the *Legend of
Thisbe* can be read profitably with *Troilus and Criseyde* in mind,
because the story of Pyramus and Thisbe appears to have been
chosen for this collection precisely because it contains similarities in theme to the poet's earlier treatment of love and its at-
tendant misfortunes. Indeed, it is possible to see the *Legend of
Thisbe* as a diminutive *Troilus and Criseyde* in theme, a retelling
of that poem intended to allow readers like the God of Love
further opportunity to understand its issues.

The two works have many similarities of plot—forced sepa-
ration, illicit love, secret meetings, mistaken "deaths," and misread signs, to name a few. They also share a theme—that misfortune and tragedy can occur in love despite the essential
blamelessness of the lovers. And because the God of Love has
erred in his reading of the *Troilus* by forcing blame on Cri-

seyde, thus missing the poem's philosophical tragedy, Chaucer cleverly demonstrates the limitations of this reading by telling what is very nearly the same story but with one significant difference—Pyramus is given a "true Criseyde." In other words, the *Legend of Thisbe* relates a tragedy in which no single character can be blamed for the misfortunes that occur. Yet in this "retelling" of the *Troilus*, we learn that the tragic consequence of earthly love is still the same with or without a culpable character; in fact, one might say that it is greater, for love causes the downfall of two lovers rather than one.

Thisbe, then, is a corrective to the God of Love's reading of the *Troilus* in several ways. It suggests that poems like the *Troilus* ought to be read not simply as exempla, as some readers had supposed. Tragedy can occur despite the "goodness" the God of Love demands from his stories. Simple accidents, such as Thisbe's loss of her veil and the complex workings of Fortune and free will in the *Troilus*, are often prime causes of earthly tragedy in love. Even faithful lovers can meet disastrous ends; two "goods" can result in a "bad." Both the *Troilus* and *Thisbe* illustrate the limitations of a narrowly moral reading of human affairs, which are complicated not only by chance and circumstance, but also, as Chaucer shows, by faulty human perception such as Pyramus's belief that blood on a wimple means his lady's death[33] or Troilus's belief that his beloved lady is the sacred shrine of a true religion.

The *Legend of Thisbe* is recognized as one of Chaucer's most literal renderings of an Ovidian text.[34] He has faithfully preserved Ovid's original, including some of the Roman poet's exaggerated rhetorical flourishes, such as the ghastly image of Pyramus's blood spurting out as if it were water from a broken conduit (851–52). In other words, with this legend Chaucer is

---

[33]In Stephen Scrope's *The Epistle of Othea*, ed. Curt F. Bühler, EETS e.s. 264 (Oxford: Oxford Univ. Press, 1970), pp. 49–51, the Pyramus and Thisbe story is moralized as a warning to its readers to beware of misinterpreting evidence as Pyramus did.

[34]See Shannon, *Chaucer and the Roman Poets*, p. 190.

playing the role of translator rather than devious falsifier of others' truths. With the exception of his appended moralizations (which do little to alter the significance of Ovid's own story), Chaucer has remained faithful to his source. Thus the *Legend of Thisbe*, while ostensibly fulfilling the requirements of the God of Love's project, nevertheless simultaneously undermines the validity of the regulations he has imposed upon the narrator's literary enterprise. Moreover, if he approves this narrative, the God of Love unknowingly admits that his judgment of the *Troilus* has been inadequate and that his sole assumption regarding human love (that tragedy in love occurs because of an unfaithful partner) ignores the wide range of human experience that literature can reflect. Chaucer's decision to include *Thisbe* and, on top of that, to translate it accurately, constitutes rebellion against the doctrines he knows are unwise.

Like *Thisbe*, the *Legend of Phyllis* contains much close translation from Ovid's *Heroides*. Chaucer's brief summary of her story repeats the now familiar pattern of betrayal, as well as the hagiographical device of recalling Alceste's precedent with the lines that describe Phyllis as "fayrer on to sene/Than is the flour ageyn the bryghte sonne" (2425–26). This summary is handled with great dispatch to leave space for her long letter, whose eloquence proves her a capable narrator of her own misfortunes. The narrator mentions that he regretfully cannot include this letter in its entirety because of the God of Love's demand for brevity:

> But al hire letter wryten I ne may
> By order, for it were to me a charge;
> Hire letter was ryght long and therto large.
> But here and ther in rym I have it layd,
> There as me thoughte that she wel hath sayd.
> [2513–17]

But despite his radical shortening of Ovid's original, Chaucer has nevertheless managed to let Phyllis's voice dominate her own legend.[35] In this sense, as he himself might be humorously boasting in the last lines of this story, he is a faithful man (both to Phyllis and to Ovid), clearly more trustworthy than the poetic villains who may have neglected her pain in their works, or may have exalted her deceiver Demophoon for his other adventures:

> Be war, ye wemen, of youre subtyl fo,
> Syn yit this day men may ensaumple se;
> And trusteth, as in love, no man but me.
>
> [2559–61]

Chaucer, though unable to prove his fidelity as an actual lover, is nevertheless faithful to the classical female lovers (if not always to the facts of their lives) this collection is designed to serve. And as a mark of his loyalty to Phyllis, he echoes her last wish—that Demophoon's betrayal of her be described truthfully in future accounts of his life:

> And whan thyne olde auncestres peynted be,
> In which men may here worthynesse se,
> Thanne preye I God thow peynted be also
> That folk may rede, forby as they go,
> "Lo! this is he, that with his flaterye
> Bytraised hath and don hire vilenye
> That was his trewe love in thought and dede!"
>
> [2536–42]

Phyllis's concern with the preservation of truth in all subsequent records of Demophoon's illustrious and heroic family brings us to one of Chaucer's own major concerns in the *Legend of Good Women* as a whole. In writing these legends, he has been

---

[35]Gavin Douglas, in the *Palice of Honour* 2.808–25, suggests strongly that the ladies of Ovid's epistles are themeselves capable poets. About them he writes, "I had greit wonder of thay Ladyis seir,/ Quhils in that airt micht have na compeir;/ Of castis quent, Rethorik colouris fine,/ Sa Poeit like in subtell fair maneir/ And eloquent firme cadence Regulair" (*The Shorter Poems of Gavin Douglas*, ed. Priscilla J. Bawcutt, Scottish Text Society, ser. 4, no. 3 [Edinburgh: Blackwood and Sons, 1967]).

keenly aware of how easy it is for a poet to magnify or diminish a human reputation simply by exercising poetic legerdemain. Moreover, he realizes that there is nothing mystical about poets creating illusions of truth; doing so merely involves the use of everyday literary skills such as cutting, expanding, editing, moralizing, or choosing the right authorities on which to base one's tale. Thus the stability of literary fame is theoretically always in question, since one's fate depends solely on the vacillating and unpredictable decisions of poets. Criseyde's painful realization of this fact resulted in her fear that she would be condemned in subsequent versions of her story, a fate that actually came to pass in the works of Henryson and Shakespeare. Like Criseyde, Phyllis realizes that her literary future is likely to hold a far worse betrayal of her than could be caused by any unfaithful man.

Chaucer's deepest involvement with this issue occurs in the *House of Fame*, a work very pertinent to the *Legend* because in it we see two conflicting versions of a story. In the *House of Fame*, Virgil's *Aeneid* and Ovid's *Heroides* vie for the honor of transmitting to posterity the love story of Aeneas and Dido. Only Virgil's account of this story seems to appear on the glorious walls of Venus's temple, but by the time the narrator has finished describing the love affair as it appears there, he has managed to introduce, in some detail, the Ovidian perspective as well. The result is a ludicrous, hybrid version of the Dido/Aeneas story which manifests radical inconsistencies in point of view, as might be expected from such a hasty amalgam of two poets with very different sympathies. Virgil's Aeneas appears as a responsible hero, Ovid's as a thoughtless deceiver, and both of these judgments get equal transmission in the *House of Fame*, thus allowing little possibility of arriving at objective truth in this matter.

However comic this mixed rendition of the story may seem, there is something to be said for Chaucer's conscious desire to record a side of the story that did not have an epic tradition to help secure its survival—namely, the Ovidian perspective that favors Dido's emotional tragedy in the face of Aeneas's departure from her. Ovid's partiality to Dido, when combined with Virgil's whole-hearted approval of his hero, makes for an inorganic and confusing narrative, but one that nevertheless succeeds in achieving a measure of fairness uncharacteristic of any previous version of the story. Chaucer, then, sets himself up as the Ovidian challenger of Virgil's one-sided case, working not to destroy what Virgil had left to posterity but simply to provide an alternative to it. With this in mind, the *House of Fame*'s narrator alludes to the tragedies of other ladies whom Ovid had rescued from literary neglect, including some of those who appear in Chaucer's legendary, such as Phyllis, Hypsipyle, Medea, and Ariadne.[36]

There is an important difference, however, between the ways in which these two works represent the classical people with whom they are concerned. In the *House of Fame*, Virgil never gets completely upstaged by the silly, impassioned narrator who introduces Ovid's viewpoint; after all, it is Virgil's account—not Ovid's—which was chosen by Venus to adorn her walls for eternity. Thus Aeneas is not likely to lose his reputation as a flawless hero merely because of the alternative opinion offered by the narrator as he scans the images about him. But in the *Legend of Good Women*, Aeneas is not shown the courtesy of fair representation (even though he is given equal time), nor are any of the other men, many of whom deserve much better treatment than they receive in the *Legend*'s short summaries. Demophoon, for example, is badly misrepresented, for in many versions of his affair with Phyllis, he returns to her after a delay, only to find that she hanged herself prematurely.[37] Therefore she only *imagined* that he was false, because he was unable to honor the prearranged date of his homecoming. This accident, of course, in no way lessens Phyllis's trag-

---

[36]See the *House of Fame* 388–426, and Fyler, pp. 32–41 and 111–13, for the Chaucerian conflicts between Virgil and Ovid.

[37]In Gower's *Confessio Amantis*, Demophoon forgets about Phyllis, but later repents his forgetfulness and returns to find her dead (4.874–78). Boccaccio, however, in the *Genealogia*, mentions Demophoon's later return but does not say that he was guilty of any neglect.

edy; she is as convinced as other ladies whose betrayals were real that she is a victim of deceit and dishonesty. She is therefore justified in desiring an honest appraisal of her fidelity to her lover, which she showed in "thought and deed." But Demophoon clearly suffers in Chaucer's (and Ovid's) hands, and one is inclined to ponder the terrible misunderstanding that might have been perpetuated if Phyllis's last wish—to see Demophoon permanently drawn as a villain—had been honored by all artists everywhere. In other words, the full artistic accommodation of one viewpoint often entails the conscious neglect of another. Thus we see that the Chaucer who is so faithful to the women in this legendary is at the same time the faithless betrayer of its men. Such is the travesty the ignorant God of Love has made of Chaucer's art in his demand that it be rid of the so-called chaff of honesty, fairness, and perspicacity. For once a literary artist is handed a set of predetermined conclusions regarding human culpability, he has no choice in the course of his narrative but to commit the injustices necessary to lead him there. In an age of moralized exempla, when literary appetites demand gratification in the form of a simple dialectic, an artist must work hard to make his stories confirm the expectations that await them, even if it means he must deface the images chosen by Fame to adorn the walls of Venus's temple.

Chaucer's awareness that he is contradicting traditional opinion is nowhere more evident than in the *Legend of Dido*. Chaucer opens his narrative by praising Virgil and by announcing the *Aeneid* as the story's main source:

> Glorye and honour, Virgil Mantoan,
> Be to thy name! and I shal, as I can,
> Folwe thy lanterne, as thow gost byforn,
> How Eneas to Dido was forsworn.
>
> [924–27]

But as in the *House of Fame*, the poet plans to introduce Ovidian elements into this Virgilian tale:

> In Naso and Eneydos wol I take
> The tenor, and the grete effectes make.
>
> [928–29]

To synthesize these two versions of the story, however, Chaucer must make some important changes in Virgil's text, one of which occurs in the scene describing the temple in which Dido and Aeneas first meet. In the *Aeneid*, the hero finds pictures painted on the temple walls which recall to him his suffering and fortitude in the Trojan War (1.456–63). He remarks to one of his companions that these pictures, powerful in their evocation of Trojan heroism, could ensure them a measure of safety in their travels because they present such a moving account of the losses of war that people will honor or pity the men shown there. Chaucer's re-creation of this scene involves some very subtle changes in its significance. Most important, he has altered the effect these images have on Aeneas, making them convey shame to him rather than glorious fortitude:[38]

> And whan this Eneas and Achates
> Hadden in this temple ben overal,
> Thanne founde they, depeynted on a wal,
> How Troye and al the lond destroyed was.
> "Allas, that I was born!" quod Eneas;
> "Thourghout the world oure shame is kid so wyde,
> Now it is peynted upon every syde.
> We, that weren in prosperite,
> Been now desclandered, and in swich degre,
> No lenger for to lyven I ne kepe."
>
> [1023–32]

Whatever Aeneas's reaction might imply about what the images on the wall actually depict, it is clear that what he sees there somehow causes him shame. Aeneas judges this particular account of the Trojan story as nothing but slander, suggesting ei-

---

[38]R. W. Frank has also observed this alteration, but he draws a different conclusion from it. See *Chaucer and the Legend of Good Women*, p. 74.

ther that the creator of these images was lying or that he told the true story in such a way as to misrepresent Aeneas and his fellow soldiers. The "desclandered" Trojans, with good reputations lost, are now permanently enshrined in the cultural memory as disgraceful losers. In making this change, Chaucer demonstrates the awesome control artists have over human destiny and reputation. Moreover, through changing the pictures on the wall, he cleverly depicts his own adjustments of Virgil's historical truth: what Aeneas sees on the wall is exactly what the readers of this slanderous legend will see—a shameful betrayer instead of a hero. And ironically, both Aeneas's concern for his good reputation and his willingness to die because of its loss are actually Dido's feelings about herself, if we are to believe the *Heroides*, the *Aeneid*, and Chaucer's *House of Fame*:

> "O, wel-awey that I was born!
> For thorgh yow is my name lorn,
> And alle myn actes red and songe
> Over al thys lond, on every tonge."
> [*House of Fame*, 345–48]

In this legend, Chaucer has obviously reversed the positions of Dido and Aeneas relative to Fame, keeping Virgil's story intact only where it does not conflict with Ovid's sympathy for Dido. He can faithfully reproduce Virgil's "images on the wall," if you will, until they interfere with the legend's moral purpose, at which time it becomes necessary to deviate from his principal "auctour" and make Dido the one whom Fame has chosen to patronize:

> . . . she was holden of alle queenes flour,
> Of gentillesse, of fredom, of beaute;
> That wel was hym that myghte hire ones se;
> Of kynges and of lordes so desyred,
> That al the world hire beaute hadde yfyred;
> She stod so wel in every wightes grace.
> [1009–14]

This expansive praise for Dido is not in itself a radical departure from Virgil, but when Chaucer implies that the Trojan lords seek her help solely *because of* her fame ("Swich renoun was there sprongen of hire goodnesse" [1054]), then he is obviously stretching Virgil's text.

Chaucer exhibits another tendency in the *Legend of Dido* which must be briefly noted. He is extremely reluctant to include in his version any of Virgil's accounts of supernatural interference, especially when that interference somehow affects the relationship between the two main characters. For example, he is unwilling to blame Venus and Cupid for initiating Dido's love for Aeneas:

> But natheles, oure autour telleth us,
> That Cupido, that is the god of love,
> At preyere of his moder hye above,
> Hadde the liknesse of the child ytake,
> This noble queen enamored to make
> On Eneas; but, as of that scripture,
> Be as be may, I take of it no cure.
>
> [1139–45]

Similarly, the storm that forces them into a cave together is a natural event in Chaucer's version but a contrivance plotted by Juno and Venus in the *Aeneid*.[39] Jove's connection with Iarbas is never mentioned by Chaucer, nor does he place much faith in Virgil's account of Aeneas's entering the temple at Carthage hidden in a cloud:

> I can nat seyn if that it be possible,
> But Venus hadde hym maked invysible—
> Thus seyth the bok, withouten any les.
>
> [1020–22]

Finally, Chaucer entirely omits Virgil's long description of Mercury's appearance before Aeneas to deliver the message that

---

[39]On the natural storm, see Shannon, p. 203. Fyler has also commented on Chaucer's editing out of supernatural elements, and he draws conclusions similar to mine. See *Chaucer and Ovid*, pp. 112–13.

the hero must leave for Italy (*Aen.* 4.238–78). In its place, Chaucer has Aeneas pretend that he learned all this in a dream—a notoriously unreliable source of information even if we could be certain that the now bored Aeneas was not simply making it up to deceive his newfound queen. It becomes clear that all of these curious alterations Chaucer made in his Virgilian text contribute to a single intention: by banishing supernatural interference in the lives of his characters, Chaucer is better able to assign blame to them and thus to make the moral judgment we have come to expect, that Aeneas is an unmercifully evil man who has full control over his own sinful behavior.

The *Legend of Dido* is certainly a coherent narrative, unlike the *House of Fame*'s version of this same love story, but readers hardly need anyone to point out to them what Chaucer has sacrificed to achieve that coherence. He has worked hard at the task of blackening Aeneas's reputation, largely by subtle revision of those Virgilian episodes that are in conflict with his intended purpose. Yet at the same time, he has retained a degree of fidelity to his sources, since he cannot be accused of independently creating any of this narrative's episodes. Even with such clever appropriation of the personae of two classical poets—Virgil and Ovid—Chaucer has nonetheless managed to tell a tale that is distinctly anomalous in its tone and significance. This legend, like others in the collection, brilliantly parodies the unfortunate results of so many medieval retellings of classical stories, especially those that are told to fit a prearranged context or to confirm some a priori system of morality. To be sure, the practice of making saints out of pagan lovers is a greatly exaggerated example of literary falsification, yet it is close enough to actual medieval practice to be classified as parody.

The God of Love is certainly justified in wishing to glorify ancient achievements, especially Alceste's, that have the power to teach us about the depth and truth of human love. But in demanding that she be set up as the "calendier," or model, for all the other ladies, he is grossly unfair. His directive to the poet, that

". . . of Alceste shulde thy wrytynge be,
Syn that thow wost that calendier is she
Of goodnesse. . . ."[40]

[G 532–34]

suggests a plan that is bound to fail, because with Alceste as the standard by which feminine truth in love is to be measured, the other ladies, as good as they are, can only suffer in comparison to her life of perfect charity. Although the ladies' lives are written to conform to her archetypal example, we must always realize the major differences between them and Alceste. Chaucer's "good women" vainly sacrificed themselves for unworthy causes, and because suicide resulting from despair does not deserve resurrection, they were not given life again by a herculean judge. The men they "saved" or died for were not devoted husbands like Alceste's Admetus, but, as Chaucer's legends would have it, merely fickle lovers whose motives were suspect from the start. Finally, many of the ladies had biographies badly in need of editing by anyone seeking to redeem them from charges of general moral turpitude. They are, without question, far inferior to Alceste if one wishes to measure them by a Christian standard of morality. For these and other reasons, the project of the legendary, designed specifically to please the God of Love, disproves his assumptions once it is carried out. His desire to have literature that is simple, unambiguous in its moral force, and part of an endless repetition of the same witless themes results in a "hagiographical classicism" that is patently unworkable. On top of that, his requirement that Christian charity and pagan eros be reconciled forces Chaucer to produce a "martyrology of love" that does little more than violate the true character of his sources.

Oddly enough, the ladies whose stories are told in this poem do not sustain the kinds of injuries we might expect of participants (and victims) in this typical Chaucerian mockery. The poet often seems quite moved by their predicaments, con-

---

[40]The F version is slightly different: "And wost so wel that kalendar ys shee/To any woman that wol lover bee" (F 542–43).

veying in some instances true compassion and sympathy. In this regard, Chaucer is imitating Ovid, especially the sophisticated narrator so visible in the *Heroides*, where the poet's ludicrous bombast and brilliant rhetorical parody are mixed with unmistakable tenderness and pity for the female victims he describes. Like Ovid, Chaucer finds his target solely in the literary forms and techniques that traditionally serve as vehicles for human experiences, not in the characters who represent those experiences.[41] We must bear in mind that throughout his legendary, Chaucer is attacking narrative strategies, not saints or classical lovers. The ladies of antiquity are not sacrificed at the God of Love's altar, even though their lives fall short of Alceste's ideal model. By telling their stories in many of Ovid's own sympathetic words, Chaucer has taken it upon himself to reward the women with the literary afterlife they all deserve. And as for the men, whose good reputations were never in question before the God of Love asked Chaucer to blacken them in his penance, they do not suffer an enduring wound either. Chaucer's gross betrayal of them in this poem is so obviously what makes the legendary "bad art" that readers are never in danger of taking seriously its views on male culpability. For, as the *Troilus* tells us, blame is not what art is all about.

[41] The Ovidian and the Chaucerian narrators share several features that are instructive to compare. Howard Jacobson, in *Ovid's Heroides* (Princeton, N.J.: Princeton Univ. Press, 1974), has shown, for example, that the *Heroides* are in some ways narratives that experiment with the "reductionist tendency" of individuals to view history from a single perspective (pp. 353–54). He also describes Ovid's interest in the "archetypal structure" of myth, the recurrent patterns that appear in the subject matter he treated (pp. 376–80). For other relationships between Chaucer and Ovid as narrators, Fyler's *Chaucer and Ovid* is the most thorough and expert study. For Ovid's interest in "parallelism" and "repetition" in literature, see also Brooks Otis, *Ovid as an Epic Poet* (Cambridge, Mass.: Harvard Univ. Press, 1970).

— 5 —

"Poesye," "Makyng,"
and "Translacioun"

Since the *Legend of Good Women* is incomplete and leaves no clues regarding Chaucer's plans for the other ladies to be included in his collection, it is fruitless to speculate further about the effect the total work might have conveyed. Henry Ansgar Kelly, however, after studying the lives of the ladies mentioned in Chaucer's "balade" and in his prologue to the *Man of Law's Tale*, has written convincingly about which women Chaucer might have chosen to complete his work.[1] He also reminds us that Alceste's story, because it survives in such a skeletal form in classical and medieval sources, would have been extremely difficult for Chaucer to expand into a legend. In the Prologue, the God of Love has already told it in the fullest form possible to any medieval narrator wishing to work faithfully with sources. If Chaucer were to lengthen it, he would have to invent far more than he had to for his tales of the better-known ladies.[2] But even without Chaucer's *Legend of Alceste* or a lengthy source to help us, we can define Alceste and her role in the

---

[1] *Love and Marriage in the Age of Chaucer* (Ithaca, N.Y.: Cornell Univ. Press, 1975), pp. 113–18. He mentions Penelope, Laodamia, Deianira, Hermoine, Helen, and Polyxena as likely candidates for inclusion.

[2] For Chaucer's sources for the Alcestis legend, see Kelly, p. 114, and Robinson, p. 846, n. 510.

Legend's Prologue with some precision. We can see, for example, that the details of her story, however scanty, seem to describe a perfectly realized example of "fyn lovynge" (F 544, G 534), one that holds true for Christian readers as well as the classical ones who first recognized her. She not only loves within the bounds of marriage, but she also has a reputation that will survive intact without any uncharitable falsification of her husband, Admetus, whose brush with death gave her the occasion for her sacrifice. In other words, unlike the lives of the other ladies, which Chaucer himself had to force into tedious Christian patterns, Alceste's life needs no rhetorical chicanery to make it conform to Christian ethical codes of love. Better still, her resurrection by Hercules rewards her for her great devotion in a manner that is naturally satisfying, on its literal level, to Christian readers; there is no need to append a tiresome and destructive allegory. Her natural virtue in conjunction with the literal facts of her life makes her worthy of universal acclaim.

It is thus not surprising to find that great throngs of ladies—classical and Christian alike—want Alceste to represent them in the fourteenth-century Christian world. In the Prologue, they hover around her, worshiping her as the symbol of their truth in love. We see not only the "ladyes nyntene" whom Chaucer's *Legend* would have treated, but also

> . . . of wymen swich a traas
> That, syn that God Adam hadde mad of erthe,
> The thridde part, of mankynde, or the ferthe,
> Ne wende I not by possibilitee
> Had ever in this wide world ybee;
> And trewe of love thise women were echon.
> [F 285–90]

In these women we find all the variety and diversity possible within a shared experience, that of being true in love. And all these women, each with a story to tell, want Alceste to bear the responsibility of recalling their virtue to others. As a woman, of course, she far excels them, but because she is poetry too, and is therefore able to join the universal and the particular in a powerful union, she is capable of the kind of effective representation of truth that Chaucer—and all artists—define as their mission. In describing the artist's role as a form of daisy worship, the *Legend* seeks to depict the natural sources of Chaucer's poetry. He wants to speak plainly and truthfully about his natural surroundings, which, however humble, are nonetheless nourished by the truth-giving rays of the sun. But in addition to being the diminutive daisy of the natural world, Alceste is also Thrace's queen, an identity that enables her to lend authority and respect to human experience by making it "larger than life." As both a daisy and a classical queen, Alceste perfectly dramatizes art's ability to preserve the wisdom in "olde bokes" by means of discovering in them the permanent values that relate to (in the case of true lovers, for example) the "thridde part, of mankynde, or the ferthe." But more than this, Alceste synthesizes universal human experience with authoritative "bokes" in a way that succeeds in maintaining the integrity and truth of both, unlike the God of Love, who manages to unite "experience" and "olde bokes" only by distorting works of ancient literature into exempla, with the result that both experience and authority are falsified and betrayed.

Chaucer's *Legend* even suggests that Alceste is able to improve upon the virtue expressed in non-Christian fiction. Chaucer's little "balade," sung by the narrator in F and by the ladies themselves in G, is intended to praise the ability of Chaucer's art, symbolized by Alceste, to transform the stories of virtuous people—whether from classical, Old Testament, or even legendary British times—into new forms that not only preserve these lives for the benefit of later readers but also help them find the natural place they deserve within the boundaries of Christian standards of truth and virtue. The first stanza reads:

> Hyd, Absalon, thy gilte tresses clere;
> Ester, ley thow thy meknesse al adoun;

Hyd, Jonathas, al thyn frendly manere;
Penelope and Marcia Catoun,
Mak of youre wyfhod no comparisoun;
Hyde ye youre beautes, Ysoude and Eleyne:
Alceste is here, that al that may desteyne.[3]

[G 203–9]

To be sure, Chaucer's lady outshines these virtuous people because her own inimitable beauty and virtue, as far as they are conceived in the scanty classical sources, far surpass those visible in the lives of these more conventional exemplary figures. But the point that Chaucer finally wishes to make in his "balade" is that Alceste outshines other legendary figures because her story has the power to preserve what is exemplary about the past without falsifying it as many of Chaucer's fourteenth-century contemporaries do and he himself does in his own ironic legendary. Uniting the classical and courtly worlds in an honest synthesis that does justice to the values of both, Alceste is a perfect realization of Chaucer's theory, put to practice in the *Troilus*, that Christian art can—and should—accommodate itself to subject matter that is not by nature its own, but that such accommodation must be carefully and honestly made.

This observation, that Alceste embodies Chaucer's principle of uniting classical and Christian traditions as they appear in the *Troilus*, leads naturally to the complex subject of how Chaucer viewed his own role as a teller of others' tales, a user of "thynges for to make," as Alceste proclaims in the *Legend*'s own words. I have avoided discussing the *Legend*'s place in Chaucer's poetic development until now, because in order to understand how this poem defines Chaucer's sense of himself as a user of classical material we must examine the special vocabulary he applies to his own activity as a poet both in the *Troilus* and in the *Legend* itself. The best place to begin such an examination is

[3]In the Prologue's F version, the refrain of this poem does not refer to Alceste by name, but merely calls her "my lady."

with one of the *Troilus*'s final stanzas, the enigmatic little *envoi* that serves as the first of that poem's several conclusions.[4] In these lines, Chaucer reveals his respect for the classical *auctores* whose works he hopes the *Troilus* has closely followed:

> But litel book, no makyng thow n'envie,
> But subgit be to alle poesye;
> And kis the steppes, where as thow seest pace
> Virgile, Ovide, Omer, Lucan, and Stace.
>
> [5.1789–92]

Chaucer suggests here what all of his works imply—that there is a marked distinction between "makyng" and "poesye." As modern research is beginning to make clear, this distinction was honored by most late medieval writers, and it served to differentiate "makers," that is, courtly craftsmen who wrote in the vernacular and who sought to meet the social interests of their own age, from "poets," who wrote things of permanent value in Latin (such as the classical artists mentioned in the stanza from the *Troilus*) or who otherwise significantly embodied the classical tradition in modern times, such as Dante and Petrarch.[5] In his own works, Chaucer never calls himself a "poet"; he clearly saw his poems as examples of "makyng," that is, as vernacular works designed to address local issues, even though they employed classical material in the course of doing so. Yet in the lines from the *Troilus* that articulate this distinction, Chaucer seems to be asking us to see that particular poem as something more than "makyng," something that might be measurable by—even subject to—the standards of "poesye." To Chaucer,

---

[4]For a discussion of the *Troilus*'s multiple endings, see John S. P. Tatlock, "The Epilog of Chaucer's *Troilus*," *MP*, 18 (1921), 625–26.

[5]See especially Winthrop Wetherbee, "Convention and Authority: A Comment on Some Recent Critical Approaches to Chaucer," in *New Perspectives in Chaucer Criticism*, ed. Donald M. Rose (Norman, Okla.: Pilgrim Books, 1981), pp. 79–80, and Glending Olson, "Making and Poetry in the Age of Chaucer," *Comparative Literature*, 31 (1979), 272–90. For a shorter treatment of the distinction between "makynge" and "poesye" in the *Troilus*'s conclusion, see Thomas J. Garbáty, "*Troilus* V, 1786–92 and V, 1807–27: An Example of Poetic Process," *Chaucer Review*, 11 (1977), 299–305.

the *Troilus* was the only work in his corpus that approached the greatness of classical literary achievement.

The more we study the strategies Chaucer uses in the *Legend of Good Women* to defend the *Troilus*'s artistic worth, the more we realize how pertinent his maker/poet distinction is to the *Legend*'s basic scheme. If to be a medieval poet (like Dante or Petrarch) meant to embody the classical tradition rather than merely to appropriate it to fit locally moral or social standards of the age, then we can see in the *Legend* how Chaucer attempts to prove that his *Troilus* does just that. He discredits the God of Love's view of the *Troilus* as a work that applies in any direct manner to fourteenth-century life. To underscore the God of Love's connection to "makyng" alone, Chaucer has him call the *Troilus* simply another example of that lesser, or "mad," kind of verse:

> "Hast thow nat mad in Englysh ek the bok
> How that Crisseyde Troylus forsok,
> In shewynge how that wemen han don mis?"[6]
>
> [G 264–66]

The legends, too, are "made" things, but they are more correctly categorized as examples of "makyng" than is the *Troilus*. All three characters in the *Legend*'s Prologue, including the narrator, refer to the writing of them as an activity suitable to a "maker," not a "poet." Alceste, the God of Love, and the narrator respectively, say:

> ". . . he shal maken, as ye wol devyse,
> Of wommen trewe in lovyng al hire lyve. . . ."
>
> [F 437–38, G 427–28]

> "But now I charge the, upon thy lyf,
> That in thy legende thou make of this wyf,
> Whan thou hast other smale ymaad before. . . ."
>
> [F 548–50, G 538–40]

---

[6]When referring to his own *Troilus*, the narrator at one point has a chance to use the verb "to make," but instead chooses "to write." See F 469, G 459: "They oghte rather with me for to holde,/ For that I of Creseyde wroot or tolde. . . ."

> And with that word my bokes gan I take,
> And ryght thus on my Legende gan I make.[7]
>
> [F 578–79, G 544–45]

Chaucer "made" the legends in that he reshaped classical material to fit the insignificant artistic goals set by the God of Love, specifically, to correct the misunderstood *Troilus* and to set guidelines for the behavior of fourteenth-century gentleman lovers. A "poet" would have been much less restricted in his purposes and therefore would have been able to create a work that was more universally applicable, in short, a work with lasting value. Time has in fact, borne out the point that Chaucer is making here: the *Troilus* has survived as a permanently valuable work, but the value of the legendary is much less clear and surely would have been so even if it had been a serious (rather than comic) attempt to make certain classical lives conform to Christian standards.

But Chaucer is not interested in merely providing us with a convenient two-term classification by which all literature might be judged. To be sure, the passage from the *Troilus* does indeed give us these two categories, "makyng" and "poesye," and even suggests that they be viewed in opposition to one another. But read more carefully, the passage clearly implies that a *tertium quid* is possible, something between "poesye" and "makyng":

> . . . litel book, no makyng thow n'envie,
> But subgit be to alle poesye. . . .
>
> [5.1789–90]

Chaucer says here that the *Troilus* should not be viewed as in any way "envious" of the success of a "maker's" work. If it is a "made" thing, it is clearly a rank above the usual courtly variety. Instead, the *Troilus* ought to be viewed as a poem that "envies," if you will, the achievements of the classical past. Coming well after the "poesye" of classical artists (who figure so largely

---

[7]The G version has the narrator awaken in these lines, the first of which reads: "And with that word, of slep I gan awake" (G 544).

in the stanza's following lines) the *Troilus* is nevertheless "subgit
to" the highest standards by which literary art can be judged:

> And kis the steppes, where as thow seest pace
> Virgile, Ovide, Omer, Lucan, and Stace.[8]
>
> [5.1791–92]

Chaucer's deliberately equivocal classification of his *Troilus*
as a work that stands somewhere between "poesye" and
"makyng" is important because the *Legend* both explains and
defends this third category of verse—primarily through the
figure of Alceste. Just as the kind of art Alceste represents cannot be easily classified as either "experiential" like the common
English daisy or authoritative like Thrace's ancient queen but is
representative of both, so it cannot be easily classified as a simple illustration of either "poesye" or "makyng." Alceste cannot
be "poesye," for example, because Chaucer has altered her
story too much for her to be considered a figure straight from
antiquity. He has added details about her to make her conform
to his own design, such as her origins in the daisy and her metamorphosis into a star, a metamorphosis that is decidedly
Chaucerian—not Ovidian as one would expect if Chaucer were
attempting fidelity to the ancient *auctores*. Moreover, Chaucer's
freedom to expand her legend is made possible in part by the
fact that no extended classical source existed about her, proving her to be a less canonical representative of classical culture
than the other ladies in Chaucer's legendary. In addition, her
status as a medieval courtly lady is unmistakably clear; she feels
so comfortable with fourteenth-century courtly norms that
Chaucer is hardly out of place in praising her identity as a
daisy with the typically overblown language of courtly lovers.
On the other hand, to reduce Alceste to the category of
"makyng" would be to fail to account adequately for her classical identity, which is so deliberately and extensively portrayed
in the *Legend*'s Prologue. This classical identity, combined with

---

[8]On these lines and the ones immediately following them, see Olson, pp.
289–90, and Garbáty, 300–301.

Chaucer's immoderate praise for the "doctrine of thise olde wyse," that is, his classical masters, shows Chaucer's interest in and commitment to the literature of antiquity. Thus Alceste must be located, as the *Troilus* is, between the two categories that described medieval verse; she is neither "poesye" nor "makyng," but something in between.[9]

That Alceste (and thus the kind of poetry Chaucer wished to continue writing) has been granted a status above mere courtly "makyng" is also evident in Chaucer's use of arguments drawn from common humanistic defenses of poetry in his description and exoneration of her role as a conveyor of symbolic truth. In the first chapter, for example, we saw that the sun analogy (of which Alceste is a part) was used to show the effectiveness of symbolic expression as a vehicle for the transmission of divine truths to humans. Similarly, we discovered that Petrarch, Boccaccio, and others defended poetry's ability to express "natural" and "historical" truth.[10] Finally we noted that the theory of *translatio* propounded and disseminated the notion that good poetry was concerned with reality and was therefore defensible as a form of divine expression. These defenses of poetry were, without exception, intended to explain the utility of "poesye," particularly works by classical poets. They were never applied to the efforts of "makers," whose works were not analogous in any way to divine methods of expression, nor even comparable in function to classical texts for they were not viewed as having any necessary relationship to "nature" or "history," as did the works of the *auctores* which the humanists were intent on preserving.[11] Therefore, in defending his Alceste by means of these models and by giving her a "natural" origin in

[9]Chaucer's interest in intermediaries in this poem has already been noted. To the examples of the figure of the Virgin Mary in Alceste and to the sun analogy as an expression of artistic mediation, one might add Chaucer's reference to the "mean" of Aristotle: "vertu is the mene,/ As Etik seith" (F 165–66).

[10]Petrarch, *Coronation Oration*, trans. Wilkins, p. 1246, and Boccaccio, *Boccaccio on Poetry*, trans. Osgood, pp. 48, 79. To these writers, one should add Richard de Bury, who sees "poetry" as presenting "natural or historical truth . . . under the guise of allegorical fiction," *The Philobiblon of Richard de Bury*, trans. E. C. Thomas (New York: Cooper Square, 1966), p. 83.

[11]For this observation see Olson, 272–73, 276.

the daisy, Chaucer is clearly aligning himself—and his art—with the defense of "poesye." Moreover, Chaucer's allusion to a Dantesque model in his *Legend* implies that his Alceste was, at least in theory, capable of competing with the very real lady of one of the medieval period's few true "poets." If Dante's lady could mediate between divine truth and human understanding, so—implies Chaucer, somewhat comically— might a little English daisy.

The *Legend* presents us not only with Alceste, who fills the intermediate space between "makyng" and "poesye," but also with examples of the remaining two kinds of literary activity, "makyng" and "poesye" both. He thus provides us with a continuum of artistic possibilities stretching from the *dits* of the courtly makers to the highest achievements of Roman poets. The God of Love, of course, because he cannot transcend his courtly origins, is Chaucer's overstated example of the patchwork efforts of minor "makers"; despite the craftsmanship that went into the creation of this imaginative deity, he never manages to synthesize fully the miscellaneous classical and Christian elements out of which he was "made." Thus he cannot compete with Alceste's form of truth, even though he tries to embody a double cultural standard similar to her own. The *Legend* shows us "poesye" too, though in a much less dramatic way. The classical poets are constantly present in the legendary itself, although we are often led to recognize their presence only by noticing how far from them Chaucer has deviated in "makyng" his legends. But in addition to their presence as the basis of Chaucer's "hagioclassical" effort, their uncorrupted voices are also occasionally heard when Chaucer chooses to translate faithfully small passages from their works.

Indeed, Chaucer's conception of translation is also crucial to the *Legend*'s purpose, for in appropriating the actual voices of the "poets" Chaucer is carrying out a duty that he took as seriously as he did the creation of his own original work. Medieval translators of classical texts, Chaucer included, may ultimately have seen their efforts as related to the noble concept of *translatio studii*, a medieval concept that Ernst Robert Curtius and

Etienne Gilson have written about as a significant component of medieval historical and literary theory.[12] The transference or "carrying across" of Roman learning into later cultures was made possible primarily through the works of chroniclers and poets, whose conscious efforts to ensure the survival of classical knowledge resulted in one of the commonest features of medieval historical and literary texts—close fidelity to classical models both in accounts of contemporary history and in literary creations. With regard to the latter, most medieval poets viewed the practice of narrating others' stories as an essential part of original composition. Mastering the art of the "retold tale," especially the classical tale, was central to a poet's education, as is made evident by the extensive discussions in the *artes poetriae* of skills such as *amplificatio*, *brevitas*, *occupatio*, and other devices necessary to the teller of tales already in existence.[13] Douglas Kelly and others have shown that medieval interest in these literary skills is related to the belief that *translatio studii*, the "transference of the past to the present," was an essential function of poets. And not surprisingly, he finds that literal translation is one of the major modes of *translatio* in the medieval period.[14]

But "translation" was presumably a much more loosely defined activity for medieval poets than it is for us, since literal renderings of literary texts from one language to another are comparatively rare in the medieval period.[15] To the medieval poet, "translation" might involve the use of editorial skills such

---

[12]See Curtius, pp. 29–30, 384–85, and Etienne Gilson's *Les idées et les lettres* (Paris: J. Vrin, 1932), pp. 183–90.

[13]See, for example, Geoffrey of Vinsauf's *Documentum*, pp. 85–95, which sets forth miscellaneous advice on "treating familiar matter," and Matthew of Vendôme's section on the treatment of "material," *Ars versificatoria* 4.

[14]See Douglas Kelly, "*Translatio Studii*: Translation, Adaptation, and Allegory in Medieval French Literature," *Philological Quarterly*, 57 (1978), 287–310, and Michelle A. Freeman, *The Poetics of Translatio Studii and Conjointure: Chrétien de Troyes's Cligés*, French Forum Monographs 12 (Lexington, Ky.: French Forum, 1979).

[15]The lack of close translation may have been partially caused by Horace's advice to poets in the *Ars Poetica* that they not be "overly faithful translators" (*AP* 131–36). Matthew of Vendôme repeats this advice in the *Ars versificatoria* (4.1,2).

as cutting, expanding, rearranging, moralizing, or even radically reinterpreting. In short, to translate meant to use all the
skills Chaucer had employed during his life as an active
"maker" of his works, including the stories that make up his
legendary. Yet most of the legends exhibit two distinct kinds of
translation: the first, a loose summarization of classical plots
coupled with moral commentaries; the second, a literal *verbum
ex verbo* translation of Ovidian texts, largely (though not exclu-
sively) drawn from the *Heroides*. That we perceive the qualita-
tive differences between the effects of these two kinds of translation in the *Legend* is central to the poem's thesis, for they are
there so that we may hear how much better the voices of
"poets" sound when compared with the dominant voice of the
legendary's "maker." Furthermore, since Chaucer had always
had an independent interest in the act of translation, he used
the *Legend* as a vehicle for further adaptations of the Ovidian
voice, with which he had begun to experiment as early as 1369,
when the *Book of the Duchess* was composed.

Chaucer's self-consciousness about his function as a translator is made apparent in the *Legend* in several ways. First, as I
noted in Chapter 3, by having the God of Love object to his
translation of the *Romance of the Rose*, the poet is able to argue
openly for the distinction he saw between authors and translators. Translators preserve for posterity what "olde clerkes" have
said, and they should not be held responsible for their *auctores'*
intentions. With the *Romance of the Rose* as the test case, Chaucer could address this issue easily—which he does by having
both Alceste and the narrator speak of the role of a translator
versus that of an original creator.[16] The *Troilus*, a work more
nearly Chaucer's own, may have needed the more complex and
lengthier defense that the *Legend* gives it, but the poet's translation of the *Romance of the Rose* hardly needs such a defense.
Translators are necessary links in the transmission of the "olde
bokes" (F, G 25) whose importance Chaucer describes at length
in the *Legend's* opening lines.

---

[16]The passages in question are F 369–72, G 349–52; F 462–65, G 452–55.

Second, the G Prologue openly records Chaucer's interest in making available to English readers the narratives of the classical past:

> For myn entent is, or I fro yow fare,
> The naked text in English to declare
> Of many a story, or elles of many a geste,
> As autours seyn; leveth hem if yow leste!
> [G 85–88]

There is, of course, much irony in these lines; the legendary's maker very rarely gives us "naked texts." But these lines also attest to Chaucer's interest in exactly the task that the legends by and large fail to carry out. Since no "naked text" of Ovid had yet appeared in English,[17] and since there was no major European precedent for what Chaucer occasionally does in the legendary, that is, translate faithfully large sections from the authors whose works he otherwise corrupts, these lines testify to Chaucer's real desire to make available in English the actual words of his predecessors. Furthermore, his interest in translation is recorded in the legendary proper by means of several analogues that seem to describe the activity of "copying" or "transcribing." Philomela's translation of her horrible torture into a woven artifact stands as a praiseworthy illustration, for example, of the kind of passionate engagement an accurate copy of an experience is able to bring about.[18] When done faithfully, such "translation" can reproduce life's complex and

---

[17]Gower's *Confessio Amantis*, even if it antedates the *Legend*, is by no means "naked Ovid," though some of the renderings in that poem from the *Heroides* are well done. Gower's retellings, however, generally force moral conclusions onto the stories, and he thus attempts to carry out in a serious manner exactly what Chaucer parodies in the *Legend*.

[18]Shannon, pp. 278–79, points out that other medieval versions of the Philomela story (such as Chrétien's in the *Ovide Moralisé*) have her create "pictures" in her tapestry by which to express her story. Chaucer and Ovid both use the word "letters" (Latin *notas*) to describe what she weaves. In other words, here she is expressing herself verbally, not in images. For another analogue that depicts weavers as artists, see the opening of Book 6 of Ovid's *Metamorphoses*, in which Arachne and Pallas vie for the prize in a weaving contest. They each weave "old stories" into their tapestries, attempting to capture the mood and power of events from the mythic past.

mutable course without reducing any of its credibility or power. The same holds true in a poet's accurate translation of an effective narrative. When a poet is faithful to the spirit of his source, he is able to reproduce and convey whatever emotional power it contains. And literal translation, the method most likely to preserve an *auctor*'s original tone and intention, is carried out so skillfully in many of the legends that Ovid's genuine pity for the ladies is faithfully transmitted to Chaucer's own readers. The result of these Ovidian translations being coupled with drab summaries or dubious moral glossing is a series of stories uneven in tone and effect. Chaucer's renderings of the *Heroides* are exceptionally moving and beautiful, in comparison to which his other editorial work—his "maker" side— seems clumsy and incompetent. This juxtaposition has made many of Chaucer's legends difficult for modern readers to appraise.

Indeed, Chaucer's Ovidian translations represent the poet at his best. To dismiss the legends *in toto* is to overlook what he clearly labored over with care and in all seriousness. These six lines quoted from Medea's letter, for example, far outshine Chaucer's cursory summaries of her story, but more than that, they constitute good poetry by any standard:

> "Whi lykede me thy yelwe her to se
> More than the boundes of myn honeste?
> Why lykede me thy youthe and thy fayrnesse,
> And of thy tonge the infynyt graciousnesse?
> O, haddest thow in thy conquest ded ybe,
> Ful mikel untrouthe hadde ther deyd with the!"
> [1672–77]

Similarly, the eleven lines of Dido's letter end her legend with solemnity and grace. Ovid's Latin is closely followed there, his figurative language preserved along with the dignified tone of his original. The last couplet, a literal translation of Ovid's *"venti vela fidemque ferent"* (*Heroides* 8.8), exemplifies his ability to turn Latin into perfectly natural English verse:

"For thilke wynd that blew youre ship awey,
The same wynd hath blowe awey your fey."

[1364–65]

The same could be said of the other translations that appear in Chaucer's *Legend*. *Thisbe, Ariadne, Philomela, Phyllis,* and *Hypermnestra* contain remarkable examples of the poet's close attention to Ovid's *Heroides* and *Metamorphoses.*[19] Chaucer juxtaposes "good" poetry with "bad" because he wishes to convey to us that he is serving two masters in the *Legend*—both Ovid and the God of Love. He shows us (in a somewhat overstated way) that a dual fidelity is required of him in this poem, fidelity to the demands of a medieval audience wanting easily digestible morality and fidelity to the classical *auctores* whose narratives he depends upon in the construction of his art and whose status as "poets" he hopes himself to achieve. Moreover, he makes it known that the demands of these two masters often differ to the point of mutual exclusivity, since absolute fidelity to the God of Love will frequently entail a betrayal of his classical source. Fortunately, it is clear where Chaucer's own preferences lie. His faithful translations from classical texts, embedded in the emotional wasteland of courtly adaptation, are distinguished examples of Chaucerian sensitivity and warmth. In his hands, classical fiction can survive intact, often needing no alteration whatsoever to ensure its existence in a Christian world. The medieval urge to alter, gloss, allegorize, and edit classical narrative—in other words, the desire to intervene between it and its readers to clarify its usefulness—is rejected by Chaucer in favor of respectful preservation of the "doctrine of these olde wyse." The *Legend*'s Prologue and stories thus serve in part to explain and defend "translation" as we know it today, the scholarly activity of turning a literary text into a new language, keeping intact both mat-

---

[19]Many scholars have remarked on the fidelity and success with which Chaucer has rendered those lines of Ovid that he chose to translate. See, for example, Frank, pp. 50–51, 73, 174–75; Dodd, pp. 218, 225, 230; Meech, p. 128; and Shannon, p. 190.

ter and form. A good translation of a Latin author is literal; in fact, to use Chaucer's own metaphor, it is a form of sun following, or more precisely, sun copying.[20] With the Roman poets as the sources of ancient truth, Chaucer's transference of that truth to readers takes place by means of his daisy, which is an exact replica of the light source that nourishes it, even though the language in which these ancient truths survive is English, not Latin. His daisy may be humble, as Chaucer might describe the simplicity of his own native tongue, but it nevertheless provides readers who stroll in English gardens with all the "verray lyght" of classical antiquity. Thus Alceste, who "turned was into a dayesye" (F 512, G 500), exemplifies Chaucer's method of preserving ancient truth in his own creation.

Recognizing this additional meaning of the daisy, that it is meant to symbolize faithful translation, forces us to look more carefully at Chaucer's reasons for linking *translatio* and translation. These two concepts are paired in the *Legend*, perhaps even subtly implied to be forms of the same etymon. Both are certainly examples of a "carrying across": the first, as we recall, is a verbal transference of meaning from one subject to another; the second, a transference of a text from one language to another. What Chaucer might intend by his skillful fusion of these two concepts in the form of his daisy is that these two processes both require full recognition and respect for literalness—the unadorned, uninterpreted way things are. *Translatio* demands acknowledgment of an object's literal existence; similarly, translation requires the appreciation of and attention to the literal senses of narratives being rendered from one language to another. We have seen in the *Legend* examples of the failure to respect literalness: the God of Love, whose affinity to the natural world is tenuous indeed, and the facetious narratives in Chaucer's collection, whose relation in their final forms

[20]Note Chaucer's ironic comments in the opening lines of *Dido*, namely, that he plans to follow Virgil's lantern as he tells his own version of this tale. Translators are light followers, as it were, but in the case of *Dido*, the light has not been followed as well as it should have been and Chaucer retains only Virgil's "tenor" and "effectes grete," instead of being faithful to the work as written, details and all.

to actual classical narratives is negligible. Thus Chaucer seems to be making a general point here: that the two sources for medieval poetry—experience and past literature—must be imitated closely if the poetry is to be effective and true. Chaucer is expressing his profound belief that art finds its validity in the artist's observation of the world and in his careful reproduction of human experience as it is shown in ancient texts. That is, one might say that a faithful *translatio experientiae Romanorum*, which would depend upon close renderings of Roman texts, is comparable in value to experience itself.

Sometime between the composition of the *Legend of Good Women* and the nineteenth-century rise of critical interest in it, the attention of readers gradually turned from the legends to the Prologue alone. Certainly, as modern readers, we lost interest in the narratives, because, not seeing them as parodies, we saw them as poor poetry. But the *Legend's* audience was not always composed of readers who neglected the legendary; in fact, it appears that Chaucer's medieval admirers felt that the stories were worthy of careful attention. Lydgate, in his *Fall of Princes*, mentions the *Legend* twice, both times in reference to the narratives proper. Lydgate's own major source was Boccaccio, but he found Chaucer to be his most immediate model, for he believed his English predecessor had prepared the way for telling classical stories in English verse. About the story of Hypermnestra, Lydgate writes:

> . . . yiff ye list han cleer inspeccioun
> Off this story upon everi side
> Redith the legende of martirs off Cupido,
> Which that Chaucer, in ordre as thei stood,
> Compiled off women that were callid good.[21]
> [1. 1781–85]

And in the prologue to this collection of classical exempla, Lydgate mentions Chaucer as his "maister," whose "legende of par-

---

[21]*Lydgate's Fall of Princes*, ed. Henry Bergen, 4 vols. (Washington: Carnegie Institute, 1923).

fit hoolynesse" told stories of women who excelled in "bounte and fairnesse" (1. 329). Furthermore, among later translators, Chaucer's *Legend* was deemed a kind of prototype. Gavin Douglas, often considered the first modern translator of a classical literary work, cites Chaucer as his master in the Prologue to his *Aeneid*, saying that Chaucer could follow Virgil word for word:

> . . . venerabill Chauser, principal poet but peir,
> In hys legend of notabill ladeis said
> That he couth follow word by word Virgill,
> Wisar than I may faill in lakar stile.[22]
>
> [1. Pro. 343–46]

He does qualify his praise, though, noting that Chaucer "gretly Virgill offendit" in changing Aeneas from a hero into a false lover. And Stephen Hawes remembers Chaucer's *Legend* as an example of the poet's ability to "translate":

> And then the tragidies, so piteous
> Of the nintene ladyes, was his translation.[23]

Needless to say, Lydgate, Douglas, and Hawes, whether they got the joke or not, were admirers of Chaucer's translations, judging them to be major components of Chaucer's canon, a testimony to the effect these works had on other late medieval storytellers.

The best known praise of Chaucer as a translator—and, incidentally, as a "poet" who adopts classical themes—comes from one of his French contemporaries. Sometime after the mid-1380s, that is, after Chaucer had begun his *Legend*, Eustace Deschamps, that prolific manufacturer of *balades* and *dits amoureux*, is known to have sent Chaucer some of his poems (probably at

---

[22]David F. C. Coldwell, ed.
[23]From Hawes's *The Historie of graunde Amoure and la bell Pucel* 1554; quoted from Caroline F. E. Spurgeon's *Five Hundred Years of Chaucer Criticism and Allusion, 1357–1900*, 3 vols. (Cambridge: Cambridge Univ. Press, 1925), 1:67.

Chaucer's request) with the suggestion that Chaucer send something in return of his own. In this famous poetic request, Deschamps alludes to Chaucer's being in the process of "building a garden," and therefore in need of "plants" for it:

> Et un vergier, où du plant demandas
> De ceuls qui font pour eulx auctorisier
> A ja long temps que tu edifias. . .[24]
>
> [17–19]

[And for a garden which you have been building, you request plants from those who make verse to win reputations .]

Scholars have suggested that Deschamps's gift to Chaucer was his flower and leaf verse, since it was written around this time and was in keeping with the contemporary French taste. The "garden," then, may well have been the *Legend*'s Prologue, for which Chaucer needed the French *marguerites* to construct his own daisy. But what strikes the reader most about Deschamps's poem to Chaucer are the terms with which he praises his fellow "flower lover." Deschamps stresses Chaucer's strengths as a moralist, a rhetorician, and a philosopher, calling him, among other things, a "high poet" (31), and a "great Ovid in poetry" (3), one who "speaks briefly" (4), but one who nevertheless manages to "illuminate the kingdom of Aeneas, England" (6). Then Deschamps asks that Chaucer send him "an authentic draught from the fountain of Helicon" (21), implying that Chaucer's verse has as its deepest inspiration classical—not modern European—models. "I am Eustace," writes Deschamps, "and you shall have some of my plants, but please look with favor on these works of a schoolboy" (27–29); "in your garden I shall be nothing but a weed compared to your noble plant"

---

[24]*Oeuvres complètes*, ed. Saint-Hilaire and Raynaud, 2:138–40. For a thorough discussion of this poem, see T. Atkinson Jenkins, "Deschamps' Ballade to Chaucer," *MLN*, 33 (1918), 268–78, whose edition and translation I have consulted.

(32–34). Deschamps need not have known about Alceste (a noble plant indeed) to have written these words. It is clear, though, that he wishes to acknowledge the greatness of the classical masters as they appear in Chaucer's poetry. And to underscore Chaucer's contribution as a *translateur* of culture, one whose major contribution to English verse consisted of his introduction into England of both the French and the classical traditions, Deschamps's insistent refrain to this *balade* reads: "Grant translateur, noble Geffroy Chaucier." Although most scholars believe that the particular "translation" to which Deschamps refers was Chaucer's *Romaunt of the Rose* (alluded to in this *balade*'s second stanza), surely Deschamps is speaking in much more general terms in his refrain. Chaucer's ability as a "translator" includes his work with classical texts, to which Deschamps pays singular attention. The classical world is in Chaucer's possession, "du tout en ta baillie" (23), and other poets can only hope to embody it as often and as well as Chaucer had succeeded in doing.

In many ways, Chaucer's *Legend* confirms what critics and scholars have been reporting about the poet's works in the last decade or so. Like many of Chaucer's other poems, the *Legend* leaves us with a sense of the poet's wide vision, his tendency to take up a variety of topics in a single work, many of which at first seem only indirectly related to the issues at hand. The *Legend*, clearly existing primarily to describe and defend Chaucer's principles of classical storytelling as they had appeared in the *Troilus*, must also be viewed as a poem about metaphor, poetry's dependence on metaphor, the nature of poetic abstraction, the problems caused by readers' misunderstandings, the relation of Christian truth to secular art, translation, and the relative merits of experience and authority in our quest for knowledge. And if the poem was originally commissioned by Queen Anne (as many believe) merely to amuse or placate the ladies at court who wanted to read love stories that corrected the antifeminist clerical tradition, then Chaucer has certainly managed to convey more significant themes than one might ever think possible in a poem with such an undistinguished origin. Finally, if the *Legend* was written in response to the imposing presence of Dante, as was the *House of Fame*, then the final outcome of Chaucer's indebtedness to him is complex indeed. The *Legend* is both an irreverent and a highly comic parody of Dante's contention that ladies symbolize God, and it is an understated confession that what Dante thought was basically right. Thus in the course of addressing its single major theme, the artist's responsibilities toward his classical sources, the poem involves its readers in a number of other issues which are not all resolved, but which contribute to our sense that this poem, like Chaucer's other works, reflects the poet's full awareness of the assumptions and beliefs upon which any intellectual enterprise is based. We can see here, as in his other poems, that Chaucer is reluctant indeed to omit from his frame of reference any perspective on the truth.

If we were to argue, however, that Chaucer was guilty of a failure to focus his views and to take a strong stand on the issues his poems develop, we would be missing the point of the poet's chosen ironic mode. The *Legend*'s affirmation that classical literature is important to Christians despite its lack of explicit Christian morality can be fully documented only by Chaucer's thorough "proof," ironically yet convincingly delivered, that any other position one might hold is inadequate to the truth. Here, as elsewhere, one of Chaucer's favorite methods of debunking what he considers inferior positions is by placing them side by side with superior ones. Thus in the Prologue we find Alceste (an example of poetry that works) in direct contrast to the God of Love (an example of poetry that does not). In the legendary, we find both "good translation" and "bad translation," neither of which for many readers is ever labeled with quite the clarity they hope to find on each new reading of this unusual collection. And by parodying the medieval moral poetry within which the characters of Latin culture are forced to exist, Chaucer shows precisely why art that presents a single moral perspective is finally inadequate to the variety and richness of the "olde appreved stories," the "sondry thynges" which form the basis of the medieval storyteller's art. Even when faced with the poet's calculated indecisiveness in its extremer forms, however, Chaucer's readers never seem to leave his works with a disturbing sense that the poet is something of a schizophrenic among the otherwise single-minded group of late medieval poets who wrote with a unity of voice or purpose, such as Langland or Gower. Rather, Chaucer's readers come away from his works with a feeling of satisfaction, a sense that they have been exposed to all sides of the issues that the poet has chosen to treat. Nothing has been staged for them to serve the interests of moral clarity, as in Langland's allegorical vision, or even, as in the case of Gower, in the interests of formal coherence. It would be perhaps accurate, then, to describe Chaucer as a "multiphrenic" poet, a collector of knowledge whose apparent inconclusiveness resulted in works like the *Canterbury Tales*, which reflect, but do not always clearly choose among, the varied perspectives of his age.

Without the *Legend of Good Women*, the *Canterbury Tales* could not have had quite the richness that it does, for in the *Legend* Chaucer develops an idea that is fully and variously kept alive on the Canterbury journey: in their desire to make art applicable and useful to them, readers often go to ridiculous extremes to find in literature's fictional structures both narrow morality and exact parallelism to their own lives. The Reeve, the Miller, the Friar, the Summoner, the Wife of Bath, the Merchant, the Host, and many other pilgrims on that literary journey do to each other's complex art very nearly what the God of Love does to the *Troilus*. In this respect the *Canterbury Tales* clearly preserves the *Legend*'s concern with what can go wrong when readers are faced with texts. There is another major parallel between the *Legend* and the *Tales*, as well. One can see that the *Legend*'s "retraction" of the *Troilus* is comparable in many ways to Chaucer's real Retraction at the end of the *Tales* and his career—this time, however, before the real God and with consequences that pertain to the fate of the poet's soul. Let us remember what Chaucer had said about the *Troilus*, that his intention there was always pure:

> ". . . what so myn auctour mente,
> Algate, God woot, yt was myn entente
> To forthren trouthe in love and yt cheryce,
> And to ben war fro falsnesse and fro vice
> By swich ensample; this was my menynge."
>
> [F 470–74, G 460–64]

In his last Retraction, Chaucer tells us (and God) the same thing, that he wrote his works with good "entente": ". . . oure book seith, 'Al that is writen is writen for oure doctrine', and that is myn entente" (1083). That is, in both of these statements Chaucer expresses confidence in the ultimate truths to be found in his works, recognizing nonetheless that earthly poets like himself may not always succeed in making their doctrines clear, especially to readers who are unfit to receive literature's highest gifts.

Selected Bibliography

Aers, David. *Piers Plowman and Christian Allegory*. London: Edward Arnold, 1975.

Alain de Lille. *Anticlaudianus*. Trans. James J. Sheridan. Toronto: Pontifical Institute of Mediaeval Studies, 1973.

Allen, Judson Boyce. *The Friar as Critic*. Nashville: Vanderbilt Univ. Press, 1971.

———. *The Ethical Poetic of the Later Middle Ages: A Decorum of Convenient Distinction*. Toronto: Univ. of Toronto Press, 1982.

Aristotle. *The Works of Aristotle*. Trans. W. D. Ross. 12 vols. Oxford: Clarendon Press, 1908–52.

Augustine. *On Christian Doctrine*. Trans. D. W. Robertson, Jr. Indianapolis: Bobbs-Merrill, 1958.

———. *The City of God*. Trans. Marcus Dods. New York: Random House, 1950.

Bede. *De schematibus et tropis*. Trans. Gussie Hecht Tannenhaus. *Quarterly Journal of Speech*, 48 (October, 1962), 237–53.

Bernard Silvester. *Cosmographia*. Trans. Winthrop Wetherbee. In *The Cosmographia of Bernardus Silvestris*. New York: Columbia Univ. Press, 1973.

Bersuire, Pierre. *Reductium morale XV*. Reprinted as *Metamorphosis Ovidiana moraliter . . . explanata*. 1509. Facsim. Intro. Stephen Orgel. New York: Garland, 1979.

Boccaccio, Giovanni. *Concerning Famous Women*. Trans. Guido A. Guarino. New Brunswick, N.J.: Rutgers Univ. Press, 1963.

——. *The Corbaccio.* Trans. Anthony K. Cassell. Urbana: Univ. of Illinois Press, 1975.

——. *Boccaccio on Poetry: Being the Preface and the Fourteenth and Fifteenth Books of Boccaccio's Genealogia Deorum Gentilium.* Trans. Charles G. Osgood. Princeton, N.J.: Princeton Univ. Press, 1930; rpt. Indianapolis: Bobbs-Merrill, 1956.

Burlin, Robert. *Chaucerian Fiction.* Princeton, N.J.: Princeton Univ. Press, 1977.

Burrow, John. *Ricardian Poetry.* London: Routledge and Kegan Paul, 1971.

Chaucer, Geoffrey. *The Works of Geoffrey Chaucer.* Ed. F. N. Robinson. 2d. ed. Boston: Houghton Mifflin, 1957.

Chenu, M.-D. "*Involucrum*: Le mythe selon les théologiens médiévaux." *AHDLMA,* 22 (1956), 75–79.

——. *Nature, Man, and Society in the Twelfth Century: Essays on New Theological Perspectives in the Latin West.* Trans. Jerome Taylor and Lester K. Little. Chicago: Univ. of Chicago Press, 1968.

Clifford, Gay. *The Transformations of Allegory.* London: Routledge and Kegan Paul, 1974.

Colish, Marcia. *The Mirror of Language.* New Haven: Yale Univ. Press, 1968.

Copleston, F. C. *Medieval Philosophy.* New York: Harper and Row, 1961.

——. *A History of Medieval Philosophy.* New York: Harper and Row, 1972.

Curtius, Ernst Robert. *European Literature and the Latin Middle Ages.* Trans. Willard R. Trask. 1953; rpt. New York: Harper and Row, 1963.

Dante Alighieri. *Convivio.* In *Literary Criticism of Dante Alighieri,* trans. Robert S. Haller. Lincoln: Univ. of Nebraska Press, 1973.

David, Alfred. *The Strumpet Muse: Art and Morals in Chaucer's Poetry.* Bloomington: Indiana Univ. Press, 1976.

de Bury, Richard. *The Philobiblon of Richard de Bury.* Trans. E. C. Thomas. New York: Cooper Square, 1966.

Delany, Sheila. *Chaucer's House of Fame: The Poetics of Skeptical Fideism.* Chicago: Univ. of Chicago Press, 1972.

Delehaye, Hippolyte. *The Legends of the Saints: An Introduction to Hagiography.* Trans. V. M. Crawford. 1907; rpt. South Bend, Ind.: Univ. of Notre Dame Press, 1961.

Denomy, Alexander J. "The Two Moralities of Chaucer's *Troilus and*

Criseyde." In *Chaucer Criticism, II: Troilus and Criseyde and the Minor Poems*. Ed. Richard J. Schoeck and Jerome Taylor. South Bend, Ind.: Univ. of Notre Dame Press, 1961, pp. 147–59.

Deschamps, Eustache. *Oeuvres complètes de Eustache Deschamps*. Ed. le marquis de Queux de Saint-Hilaire and Gaston Raynaud. Société des anciens textes français. 11 vols. Paris, 1878–1904.

Dodd, William G. *Courtly Love in Chaucer and Gower*. Boston: Ginn, 1913.

Donatus. *Ars grammatica*. In *Grammatici Latini*, ed. H. Keil. 7 vols. Leipzig, 1855–70.

Douglas, Gavin. *The Shorter Poems of Gavin Douglas*. Ed. Priscilla J. Bawcutt. Scottish Text Society. Ser. 4, no. 3. Edinburgh: Blackwood and Sons, 1967.

———. *Virgil's Aeneid*. Ed. David F. C. Coldwell. Scottish Text Society. No. 25. Edinburgh: Blackwood and Sons, 1957.

Dunbar, H. Flanders. *Symbolism in Medieval Thought and Its Consummation in the Divine Comedy*. New Haven: Yale Univ. Press, 1929.

Estrich, Robert M. "Chaucer's Maturing Art in the Prologues to the *Legend of Good Women*." *JEGP*, 36 (1937), 326–37.

———. "Chaucer's Prologue to the *Legend of Good Women* and Machaut's *Le Jugement dou Roy de Navarre*." *SP*, 36 (1939), 20–39.

Faral, Edmond, ed. *Les arts poétiques de XIIe et XIIIe siècles*. Paris: Lib. Honoré Champion, 1958.

Fleming, John V. *The Romance of the Rose: A Study in Allegory and Iconography*. Princeton, N.J.: Princeton Univ. Press, 1969.

Fletcher, Angus. *Allegory: The Theory of a Symbolic Mode*. Ithaca, N.Y.: Cornell Univ. Press, 1964.

Frank, Robert Worth, Jr. *Chaucer and the Legend of Good Women*. Cambridge, Mass.: Harvard Univ. Press, 1972.

Freeman, Michelle A. *The Poetics of Translatio Studii and Conjointure: Chrétien de Troyes's Cligés*. French Forum Monographs 12. Lexington, Ky.: French Forum, 1979.

Froissart, Jean. *Oeuvres de Froissart*. Ed. Auguste Scheler. 3 vols. Brussels, 1870–72.

Fyler, John M. *Chaucer and Ovid*. New Haven, Conn.: Yale Univ. Press, 1979.

Galway, Margaret. "Chaucer's Sovereign Lady: A Study of the Prologue to the *Legend* and Related Poems." *MLR*, 33 (1938), 145–99.

Garbáty, Thomas J. "*Troilus* V, 1786–92 and V, 1807–27: An Example of Poetic Process." *Chaucer Review*, 11 (1977), 299–305.

Gardner, John. *The Poetry of Chaucer.* Carbondale: Southern Illinois Univ. Press, 1977.

Garrett, Robert Max. "'Cleopatra the Martyr' and Her Sisters." *JEGP,* 22 (1923), 64–74.

Geoffrey of Vinsauf. *Documentum de modo et arte dictandi et versificandi.* Trans. Roger P. Parr. Mediaeval Philosophical Texts in Translation. No. 17. Milwaukee, Wis.: Marquette Univ. Press, 1968.

——. *The Poetria nova.* In *The Poetria nova and its Sources in Early Rhetorical Doctrine,* ed. and trans. Ernest Gallo. The Hague: Mouton, 1971.

Gesta Romanorum. Trans. Charles Swan and revised by Wynnard Hooper. London: Bohn's Antiquarian Library, 1891.

Gilson, Etienne. *Les idées et les lettres.* Paris, J. Vrin, 1932.

Goddard, H. C. "Chaucer's *Legend of Good Women.*" *JEGP,* 7 (1908), 87–129.

——. "Chaucer's *Legend of Good Women,* II." *JEGP,* 8 (1909), 47–111.

Greenfield, Concetta Carestia. "The Poetics of Francis Petrarch." In *Francis Petrarch, Six Centuries Later.* North Carolina Studies in the Romance Languages and Literatures 3. Chapel Hill: Univ. of North Carolina Press, 1975, pp. 213–22.

Griffith, D. D. "An Interpretation of Chaucer's *Legend of Good Women.*" In *Manly Anniversary Studies.* Chicago: Univ. of Chicago Press, 1923, pp. 32–41.

Guido delle Colonna. *Historia Destructionis Troiae.* Ed. Nathaniel E. Griffin. Mediaeval Academy of America Publication 26. Cambridge, Mass.: Mediaeval Academy, 1936.

Guillaume de Lorris and Jean de Meun. *Le Roman de la Rose.* Ed. E. Langlois. 5 vols. Paris: Société des anciens textes français. 1914–24.

Haflants, M. Corneille, trans. *On the Song of Songs I. The Works of Bernard of Clairvaux.* Cistercian Fathers Series, no. 4. Spencer, Mass.: Cistercian Publications, 1971.

Hardison, O. B., Jr. *The Enduring Monument: A Study of the Idea of Praise in Renaissance Literary Theory and Practice.* 1962; rpt. Westport, Conn.: Greenwood Press, 1973.

Hirn, Yrjö. *The Sacred Shrine.* Boston: Beacon Press, 1957.

Hirsch, E. D., Jr. *Validity in Interpretation.* New Haven, Conn.: Yale Univ. Press, 1967.

Hollander, Robert. "*Vita Nuova*: Dante's Perceptions of Beatrice." *Dante Studies,* 92 (1974), 1–18.

Howard, Donald R. *The Idea of the Canterbury Tales.* Berkeley: Univ. of California Press, 1976.

Huppé, Bernard F. "Historical Allegory in the Prologue to the *Legend of Good Women.*" *MLR*, 43 (1948), 393–99.

Jacobson, Howard. *Ovid's Heroides.* Princeton, N.J.: Princeton Univ. Press, 1974.

Jacobus de Voragine. *The Golden Legend.* Trans. Granger Ryan and Helmut Ripperger. 1941; rpt. New York: Arno Press, 1969.

Jefferson, Bernard L. "Queen Anne and Queen Alcestis." *JEGP*, 13 (1914), 434–43.

Jenkins, T. Atkinson. "Deschamps' Ballade to Chaucer." *MLN*, 33 (1918), 268–78.

John of Salisbury. *Metalogicon.* Trans. Daniel F. McGarry. 1955; rpt. Gloucester, Mass.: Peter Smith, 1971.

Jones, Charles W. *Saints' Lives and Chronicles in Early England.* Ithaca, N.Y.: Cornell Univ. Press, 1947.

Kelly, Douglas. "The Theory of Composition in Medieval Narrative Poetry and Geoffrey of Vinsauf's *Poetria nova.*" *Mediaeval Studies*, 31 (1969), 117–48.

———. "*Translatio Studii*: Translation, Adaptation, and Allegory in Medieval French Literature." *Philological Quarterly*, 57 (1978), 287–310.

Kelly, Henry Ansgar. *Love and Marriage in the Age of Chaucer.* Ithaca, N.Y.: Cornell Univ. Press, 1975.

Kittredge, George L. "Chaucer's Alceste." *MP*, 6 (1908–9), 435–39.

Knopp, Sherron. "Chaucer and Jean de Meun as Self-Conscious Narrators: The Prologue to the *Legend of Good Women* and the *Roman de la Rose* 10307–680." *Comitatus*, 4 (1973), 25–39.

Knowles, David. *The Evolution of Medieval Thought.* New York: Random House, 1962.

Leff, Gordon. *Medieval Thought: Augustine to Ockham.* Baltimore: Penguin Books, 1958.

Lewis, C. S. "What Chaucer Really Did to *Il Filostrato.*" *Essays and Studies by Members of the English Association*, 17 (1932), 56–75. Rpt. in *Chaucer Criticism, II: Troilus and Criseyde and the Minor Poems.* Ed. Richard J. Schoeck and Jerome Taylor. South Bend, Ind.: Univ. of Notre Dame Press, 1961, pp. 16–33.

Lowes, John Livingston. "The Prologue to the *Legend of Good Women* as Related to the French Marguerite Poems and the *Filostrato.*" *PMLA*, 19 (1904), 593–683.

———. "The Prologue to the *Legend of Good Women* Considered in Its Chronological Relations." *PMLA*, 20 (1905), 749–864.

———. "Is Chaucer's *Legend of Good Women* a Travesty?" *JEGP*, 8 (1909), 513–69.

Lydgate, John. *The Fall of Princes*. Ed. Henry Bergen. Washington: Carnegie Institute, 1923.

Machaut, Guillaume de. *Oeuvres de Guillaume de Machaut*. Ed. Prosper Tarbé. Paris, 1849.

Macrobius. *Commentary on the Dream of Scipio*. Trans. William Harris Stahl. New York: Columbia Univ. Press, 1952.

Martianus Capella. *De nuptiis philologiae et mercurii*. Ed. F. Eyssenhardt. Leipzig: Tuebner, 1866.

Matthew of Vendôme. *Ars versificandi*. Trans. Ernest Gallo. In "Matthew of Vendôme: Introductory Treatise on the Art of Poetry." Proceedings of the American Philosophical Society 118, no. 1. Philadelphia: American Philosophical Society, 1974.

McAlpine, Monica E. *The Genre of Troilus and Criseyde*. Ithaca, N.Y.: Cornell Univ. Press, 1978.

McCall, John P. *Chaucer among the Gods*. University Park: Pennsylvania State Univ. Press, 1979.

Meech, Sanford Brown. "Chaucer and an Italian Translation of the *Heroides*." *PMLA*, 40 (1930), 110–28.

Le Ménagier de Paris. Trans. Eileen Power. London: Routledge and Sons, 1928.

Migne, J. P., ed. *Patrologiae cursus completus*: *Series Latina*. 221 vols. Paris: J. P. Migne, 1844–65.

Moore, Samuel. "The Prologue to Chaucer's 'Legend of Good Women' in Relation to Queen Anne and Richard." *MLR*, 7 (1912), 488–93.

Mosher, Joseph Albert. *The Exemplum in the Early Religious and Didactic Literature of England*. New York: Columbia Univ. Press, 1911.

Murphy, James J. "A New Look at Chaucer and the Rhetoricians." *RES*, 15 (1964), 1–20.

———. *Rhetoric in the Middle Ages*. Berkeley: Univ. of California Press, 1974.

Murrin, Michael. *The Veil of Allegory*. Chicago: Univ. of Chicago Press, 1969.

Neilson, William Allan. *The Origins and Sources of the Court of Love*. Studies and Notes in Philology and Literature 6. Boston: Ginn, 1899.

Nelson, William. *Fact or Fiction: The Dilemma of the Renaissance Storyteller*. Cambridge, Mass.: Harvard Univ. Press, 1973.

Nemetz, Anthony. "Literalness and the *Sensus litteralis.*" *Speculum*, 34 (1959), 76–89.

Nims, Margaret F. "*Translatio*: 'Difficult Statement' in Medieval Poetic Theory." *University of Toronto Quarterly*, 43 (Spring, 1974), 215–30.

Nolan, Narbara. "The *Vita nuova* and Richard of St. Victor's Phenomenology of Vision." *Dante Studies*, 92 (1974), 35–52.

Olsen, Alexandra Hennessey. "'*De historiis sanctorum*': A Generic Study of Hagiography." *Genre* 13 (1980), 407–29.

Olson, Glending. "Making and Poetry in the Age of Chaucer." *Comparative Literature*, 31 (1979), 272–90.

Otis, Brooks. *Ovid as an Epic Poet.* Cambridge, Mass.: Harvard Univ. Press, 1970.

Owst, G. R. *Literature and Pulpit in Medieval England.* 2d ed. 1933; rpt. Oxford: Blackwell, 1961.

Panofsky, Erwin. *Studies in Iconology.* 1939; rpt. New York: Harper and Row, 1972.

Payne, Robert O. *The Key of Remembrance: A Study of Chaucer's Poetics.* New Haven, Conn.: Yale Univ. Press, 1963.

Pelikan, Jaroslav. *The Growth of Medieval Theology (600–1300).* Chicago: Univ. of Chicago Press, 1978.

Petrarch, Francis. *Coronation Oration.* Trans. E. H. Wilkins. "Petrarch's Coronation Oration." *PMLA*, 68 (1953), 1241–50.

Piehler, Paul. *The Visionary Landscape: A Study in Medieval Allegory.* London: Edward Arnold, 1971.

Preminger, Alex, O. B. Hardison, Jr., and Kevin Kerrane, eds. *Classical and Medieval Literary Criticism: Translations and Interpretations.* New York: Frederick Ungar, 1974.

Quain, Edwin A. "The Medieval *Accessus ad Auctores.*" *Traditio*, 3 (1945), 215–64.

Quilligan, Maureen. *The Language of Allegory: Defining the Genre.* Ithaca, N.Y.: Cornell Univ. Press, 1979.

Quintilian. *Institutio oratoria.* Ed. and trans. H. E. Butler. 4 vols. New York: G. P. Putnam's, 1921.

Rhetorica ad Herennium. Ed. and trans. Harry Caplan. Cambridge, Mass.: Harvard Univ. Press, 1968.

Robertson, D. W., Jr. *A Preface to Chaucer: Studies in Medieval Perspectives.* Princeton, N.J.: Princeton Univ. Press, 1962.

Root, Robert K. "Chaucer's Legend of Medea." *PMLA*, 24 (1909), 124–53.

——. *The Poetry of Chaucer.* Boston: Houghton Mifflin, 1922.

——, ed. *Troilus and Criseyde*. Princeton, N.J.: Princeton Univ. Press, 1926.

Rose, Donald M., ed. *New Perspectives in Chaucer Criticism*. Norman, Okla.: Pilgrim Books, 1981.

Schoeck, Richard J. and Jerome Taylor, eds. *Chaucer Criticism, II: Troilus and Criseyde and the Minor Poems*. South Bend, Ind.: Univ. of Notre Dame Press, 1961.

Seznec, Jean. *The Survival of the Pagan Gods*. Trans. Barbara F. Sessions. Bollingen Series 38. Princeton, N.J.: Princeton Univ. Press, 1953.

Shannon, Edgar Finley. *Chaucer and the Roman Poets*. Cambridge, Mass.: Harvard Univ. Press, 1929.

Singleton, Charles S. *Essay on the Vita Nuova*. Cambridge, Mass.: Harvard Univ. Press, 1949.

——. *Journey to Beatrice*. Dante Studies, 2. Cambridge, Mass.: Harvard Univ. Press, 1958.

Smalley, Beryl. *English Friars and Antiquity in the Early Fourteenth Century*. Oxford: Blackwell, 1960.

The South English Legendary. Ed. Charlotte D'Evelyn and Anna Mill. 2 vols. EETS e.s. 236. London: Oxford Univ. Press, 1956.

Southern, R. W. *Medieval Humanism and Other Studies*. Oxford: Blackwell, 1970.

Spearing, A. C. *Medieval Dream-Poetry*. Cambridge: Cambridge Univ. Press, 1976.

Spenser, Edmund. *Poetical Works*. Ed. J. C. Smith and E. de Selincourt. Oxford: Oxford Univ. Press, 1970.

Spurgeon, Caroline F. E. *Five Hundred Years of Chaucer Criticism and Allusion, 1357–1900*. 3 vols. Cambridge: Cambridge Univ. Press, 1925.

Stock, Brian. *Myth and Science in the Twelfth Century: A Study of Bernard Silvester*. Princeton, N.J.: Princeton Univ. Press, 1972.

Tatlock, John S. P. "Notes on Chaucer: Earlier or Minor Poems." *MLN*, 29 (1914), 99–100.

——. "The Epilog of Chaucer's *Troilus*." *MP*, 18 (1921), 625–26.

——. "Chaucer and the *Legenda Aurea*." *MLN*, 45 (1930), 296–98.

Taylor, Beverly. "The Medieval Cleopatra: The Classical and Medieval Tradition of Chaucer's *Legend of Cleopatra*." *Journal of Mediaeval and Renaissance Studies*, 7 (1977), 249–69.

Trimpi, Wesley. "The Ancient Hypothesis of Fiction." *Traditio*, 27 (1971), 1–78.

SELECTED BIBLIOGRAPHY

Tupper, Frederick. "Chaucer's Lady of the Daisies." *JEGP*, 21 (1922), 293–317.

Tuve, Rosamund. *Elizabethan and Metaphysical Imagery.* Chicago: Univ. of Chicago Press, 1947.

——. *Allegorical Imagery.* Princeton, N.J.: Princeton Univ. Press, 1966.

Walter Map. *De nugis curialium.* Trans. Frederick Tupper and Marbury Bladen Ogle. London: Chatto and Windus, 1924.

Weese, Walter E. "Alceste and Joan of Kent." *MLN*, 63 (1948), 474–77.

Welter, J.-Th. *L'Exemplum dans la littérature religieuse et didactique du moyen age.* Paris: Occitania, 1927.

Wetherbee, Winthrop. *Platonism and Poetry in the Twelfth Century.* Princeton, N.J.: Princeton Univ. Press, 1972.

——. "Convention and Authority: A Comment on Some Recent Critical Approaches to Chaucer." In *New Perspectives in Chaucer Criticism.* Ed. Donald M. Rose. Norman, Okla.: Pilgrim Books, 1981, pp. 71–81.

Wimsatt, James I. *The Marguerite Poetry of Guillaume de Machaut.* University of North Carolina Studies in the Romance Languages and Literatures, no. 87. Chapel Hill: Univ. of North Carolina Press, 1970.

Wolpers, Theodor. *Die Englische Heiligenlegende des Mittelalters.* Tübingen: Max Niemeyer, 1964.

Woolf, Rosemary. "Saints' lives." In *Continuations and Beginnings: Studies in Old English Literature.* Ed. E. G. Stanley. London: Thomas Nelson, 1966, pp. 37–66.

Young, Karl. "Chaucer's Appeal to the Platonic Deity." *Speculum*, 19 (1944), 1–13.

Index

Library of Congress Cataloging in Publication Data

Kiser, Lisa J., 1949–
  Telling classical tales.

  Bibliography: p.
  Includes index.
    1. Chaucer, Geoffrey, d. 1400. The legend of good women. 2. Chaucer,
Geoffrey, d. 1400—Knowledge—Literature. 3. Classical literature—History
and criticism. 4. Narrative poetry—History and criticism. I. Title.
PR1882.K57   1983   821 .1   83-45135
  ISBN 0-8014-1601-9